MOUS Proficient Test Preparation: Excel 97

Acknowledgments

This edition of the workbook is based on Microsoft Excel 97. Other application versions may vary.

Product Development: Ron Pronk
Cyndi Keene

Production: Geoff Chalmers
John Chesbro
Lynn Lee
Barbara Hernandez

SES97–08221

Visit our Web site at www.activeeducation.com

Criteria for Using this Excel 97 Proficiency Workbook

- Before or after each class, insert the data diskette in the floppy drive. Open the file named "Excelprep1." When the dialog box appears, click the **Unzip** button. This will install or restore all Excel data files to the C:\Excelprep1 directory, or to the directory of your choice.

  The Practice Exercises and Test use the following files:

Book2	Regional Budget
Commissions	Sales 5
Exam Scores	Shoe company
Exam Scores 2	Test1
February Commissions	Test2
Formula Practice	Test3
More Scores	Weekly Sales
Office Totals	Work1-4
	Work6-1

Table of Contents

Preparing for the Excel Proficient Test

The Microsoft Office User Specialist (MOUS) program is a testing process sponsored by Microsoft and developed by IntraNet. The training program is designed to prepare individuals for either proficient- or expert-level knowledge of a particular Microsoft Office application. Microsoft certification at either level is often required by employers either as a condition of employment or as a condition of advancement within a company or other organization.

Test Preparation Objectives

The goal of this book is to prepare you for the Microsoft Office User Specialist proficient test. By the end of this course, you should have a strong knowledge of all proficient test topics, and should feel comfortable in your ability to pass the test.

Test-Taking Tips

The Excel Proficient exam is an all hands-on test; there are no multiple choice or other objective questions. Instructions are general in the sense that you are given basic tasks to perform on the computer but are given no help in figuring out how to perform them.

Pay *very* careful attention to instructions, though. They can be tricky. It is easy to miss some things. For instance, you might define a formula correctly but place it in the wrong cell. This would result in a lower test score. Overall, the test is quite challenging. You should practice all of your skills thoroughly in advance and look for areas of weakness that you can improve. Be aware that there is more than one exercise — use the <NEXT> button to check.

The test will be from 30 to 45 minutes in length (length varies from test to test) and you will probably need every minute of it. You are allowed to use help screens, but excessive use of them will slow you down and possibly prevent you from completing the test within the alloted time. Except for all but the most experienced users, the test preparation course is essential to completing the test correctly and within the time period allowed.

Some topics covered in this book will not appear on the test; however, they are included here to help you improve your efficiency when taking the test. For example, the Go To command is not part of the proficient test, but the topic is included here because it can help you navigate through worksheets more quickly. Most of Lesson 1 reviews basic navigation skills that should aid you in taking the test.

The test program includes a timer that begins as soon as you read the first test question, and displays continually on your monitor. The timer can be intimidating to some test takers. Microsoft does not give you much time to stumble around, so if timed tests tend to make you nervous, you should keep your eyes averted from the timer.

If you are asked to demonstrate a skill and you find that you are spending too much time in completing it, move on to the next instruction. You can always return to incomplete tasks when you have completed all of the others.

A window of instructions remains open while you take the test, but it can obstruct the view of Excel files you are working on. You cannot minimize this window. However, you can close it and reopen it or drag it down as far as possible so that it is out of the way of your file content. Be prepared for this. You can waste valuable minutes trying to figure out what to do with this window to get it out of your way. You need to refer back to the instructions on almost a continual basis, so opening and closing the instruction window frequently can also take up valuable time. The test is much easier to complete on a large monitor. In any case, the best place for the instruction window is at the bottom of the screen.

The computer notifies you when you have 10 minutes and 5 minutes left. Grading is done by the computer after you complete the test. It is pass/fail only. If you pass, a certificate will be mailed to you within a few weeks.

Starting Excel

You start Excel by first turning on your computer and monitor, and displaying the Windows 95 interface.

To start Excel:

- Click the Start button.
- Select Programs on the Start menu.
- Click Microsoft Excel on the Programs submenu to display the Excel window, as shown below:

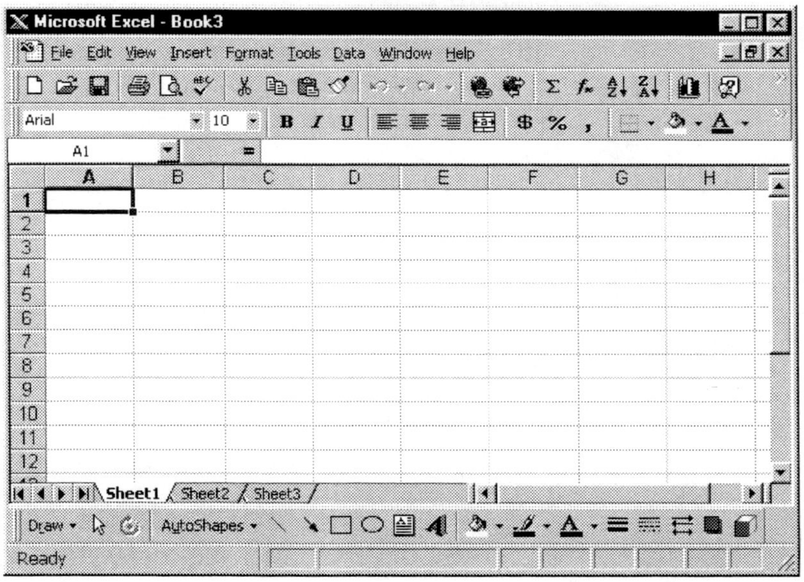

Excel Window Elements

Many elements in the Excel window are similar to other Windows 95 applications. The following describes the elements in the Excel window:

Title bar	identifies the current application being run and the name of the current workbook.
Menu bar	lists the various menus available for the current workbook window.
Toolbars	allow you to quickly perform common operations for formatting, aligning, and totaling cell entries. The Standard and Formatting toolbars appear by default. The names of the toolbar buttons appear when the mouse pointer is positioned over them.
Formula bar	displays the contents of the current cell.
Status bar	displays information about a selected command. It also indicates the status of certain keys, such as Caps Lock and Num Lock.
Scroll elements	include two scroll bars, two scroll boxes, and four scroll arrows, all of which are used to move through the window.
Select All button	selects an entire worksheet.
Sheet tabs	display the names of the worksheets within a workbook.
Tab scrolling buttons	used to scroll through the worksheets in a workbook.
Worksheet	consists of a grid of vertical columns identified by alphabetic characters, and horizontal rows identified by numeric digits. Columns and rows intersect to form cells. Each cell can be identified by a full-cell reference, or address, consisting of the column and row coordinates of that cell—for example, B3.
Active cell	the cell surrounded by a border that designates where the next item of data that you enter will appear.
Minimize button	minimizes the window to a button on the taskbar.
Close	closes the current window.

Using Cascading Menus

Cascading menus automatically flow from one option to the next, and from one menu to the next as the mouse pointer is dragged over them.

To display a menu:

- Click the menu name on the menu bar *or*

  Press [Alt] + the underlined letter of the menu name.

To select an option on a menu, either position the mouse pointer over the desired option and click it, or press the key for the underlined letter in the menu option you want. On some menus, you may find that certain selections appear dimmed. This indicates that those commands are not applicable to the current operation and, therefore, are not available at the time. Those same selections will be displayed in normal intensity as soon as they become relevant to the operation being performed.

Displaying Object Menus

Object menus are displayed by positioning the mouse pointer on an object such as a toolbar or word, then right-clicking the mouse button. A menu with the most often used commands specific to that object is displayed. Object menus will vary depending on the object that is clicked.

Using Shortcut Keys

Many Excel commands can also be executed directly from the keyboard with special shortcut keys. For example, pressing [Ctrl] + [S] is equivalent to displaying the File menu and selecting the Save command. These shortcut keys appear next to the associated commands on the pull-down menus. Many are also listed in the Lesson Summary of this workbook.

Moving Around in the Worksheet Window

To move to different cells using a mouse, simply position the mouse pointer at the desired location, and click the left mouse button.

The illustration below summarizes the keyboard methods for moving to different cells:

Press:	To move:
<Right Arrow>	right one column
<Left Arrow>	left one column
<Up Arrow>	up one row
<Down Arrow>	down one row
<Ctrl> + <Right Arrow>	to the last column in the worksheet
<Ctrl> + <Left Arrow>	to the first column in the worksheet
<Ctrl> + <Home>	to the beginning of the worksheet
<Page Up>	up one screen
<Page Down>	down one screen
<Alt> + <Page Up>	left one screen
<Alt> + <Page Down>	right one screen
<Ctrl> + <Page Down>	next worksheet page
<Ctrl> + <Page Up>	previous worksheet page

Scrolling the Worksheet

An entire worksheet contains a total of 256 columns (identified by the alphabetic characters A through Z, followed by AA through AZ, BA through BZ, and so on up to IV) and 65,536 rows. You can access cells that are not currently visible by moving, or *scrolling* the window using the scroll elements displayed below:

To scroll the worksheet window:

- by a column or row, click the left, right, up, or down scroll arrows to move one column/row in the associated direction.
- by several columns or rows, drag the horizontal or vertical scroll box along the scroll bar to move the window in the corresponding direction.
- by one full window of columns or rows, click the scroll bar (either to the left or right of the horizontal scroll box, or above or below the vertical scroll box) to move the window in the direction of the mouse pointer.

Using the Go To Command

An alternate method for quickly moving to another cell in the worksheet is using the Go To command on the Edit menu. The Go To command takes you directly to a specific cell.

To use Go To:

- Click Edit on the menu bar.
- Click Go To on the Edit menu.
- Type a cell reference in the Reference text box.
- Click the OK button.

NOTE: You can also display the Go To dialog box by pressing [F5].

Selecting a Single Cell

To select a single cell, simply click in that cell. When a cell is selected, a black border surrounds the cell, and that cell becomes the active cell.

NOTE: When you select a cell, its *row selector* (the gray button at the left end of its row) and its *column selector* (the gray button at the top of its column) both display their text in boldface. That makes it easy to see the row and column "coordinates" of the selected cell.

Selecting a Range of Cells

A *range* is normally identified by the references for its first and last cells with a colon between them. For example, the vertical range extending from cell A1 to cell A9 is identified as A1:A9. Likewise, the horizontal range extending from cell C3 to cell G3 is identified as C3:G3. Ranges that include a block of columns and rows are identified by the addresses for the cells in the upper-left and lower-right corners of that block, as displayed below:

You select a range of cells by dragging the mouse pointer over the cells. When you select a range of cells, the first cell chosen becomes the active cell.

Selecting Nonadjacent Ranges of Cells

A nonadjacent, or *noncontiguous*, range of cells consists of more than one disconnected range of cells, as displayed below:

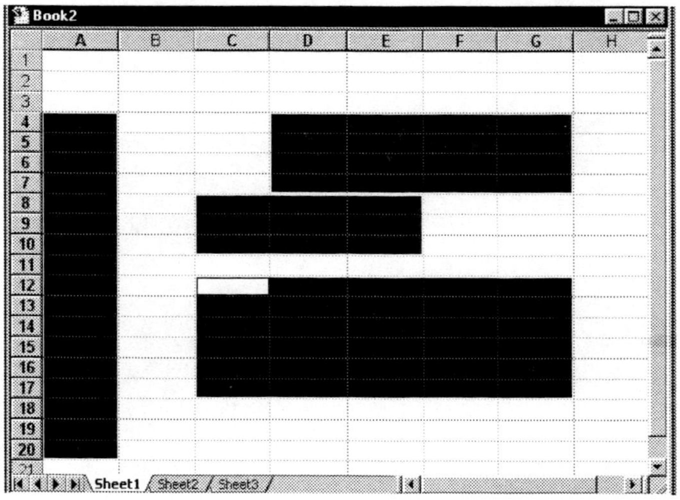

To select a noncontiguous range of cells:

- Select the first range of cells.
- Press and hold [Ctrl].
- Select the second range of cells.

Selecting Rows and Columns

You can select an entire row or column in a worksheet by clicking the corresponding row or column selector in the border, as displayed below:

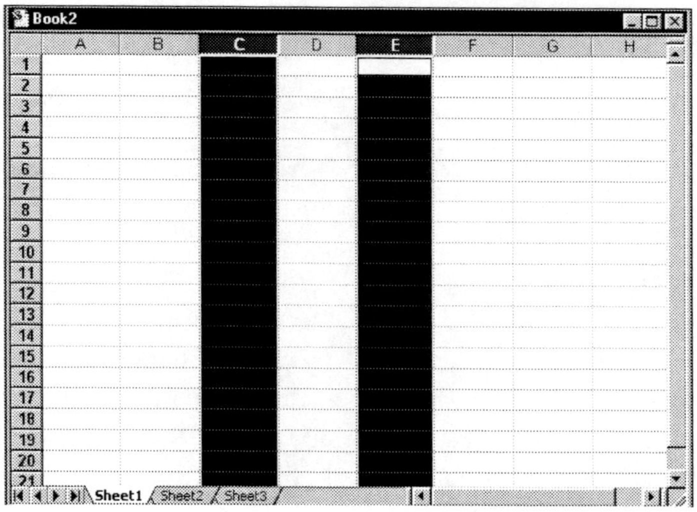

To select more than one adjacent column or row, drag the mouse pointer over the column or row selectors. To select the entire worksheet, click the Select All button at the intersection of the column and row selectors.

Summary of Lesson 1

The Office 97 installation program creates a shortcut icon for Excel and places it in the c:\Program Files\Microsoft Office folder. You can drag this icon to your desktop for easy access to the Excel program.

Shortcut	
	To start Excel: • Click the **Start** button. • Select **Programs** on the Start menu. • Click **Microsoft Excel** on the Programs submenu.
[Alt] + the underlined letter of the menu name.	**To display a menu:** • Click the menu name on the menu bar.
[Page Up] and **[Page Down]**	**To scroll the workbook window:** • by a column or row, click the left, right, up, or down scroll arrows to move one column/row in the associated direction. • by several columns or rows, drag the horizontal or vertical scroll box along the scroll bar to move the window in the corresponding direction. • by one full window of columns or rows, click the scroll bar (either to the left or right of the horizontal scroll box, or above or below the vertical scroll box) to move the window in the direction of the mouse pointer.
[Ctrl] + **[G]** *or* **[F5]**	**To use Go To:** • Click **Edit** on the menu bar. • Click **Go To** on the Edit menu. • Type a cell reference in the Reference text box. • Click the **OK** button.
[Shift] + Click a target cell to select all cells from the position of the cursor to the target cell.	**To select a continuous range of cells:** • Click and drag from the start of the range to the end of the range.

To select a noncontiguous range of cells:

- Select the first range of cells.
- Press and hold **[Ctrl]**.
- Select the second range of cells.

Practice Exercise A — Lesson 1

1. Using the Go To command, make cell CA5000 the active cell.

2. Using the scroll bars, scroll the window back to its original position, and click cell **A1**.

3. Select the following nonadjacent ranges: **A1:A10, D4:G4, C8:E12, G12:H17**.

4. Position the selector in cell A1.

Practice Exercise B — Lesson 1

1. Maximize the worksheet window.

2. Using the Go To command, make cell B75 the active cell.

3. Using the Go To command, return to the first cell in the worksheet.

4. Select the following nonadjacent ranges: **A4:A20, D4:G7, C8:E10, C12:G17**. Your worksheet should look like the one shown below:

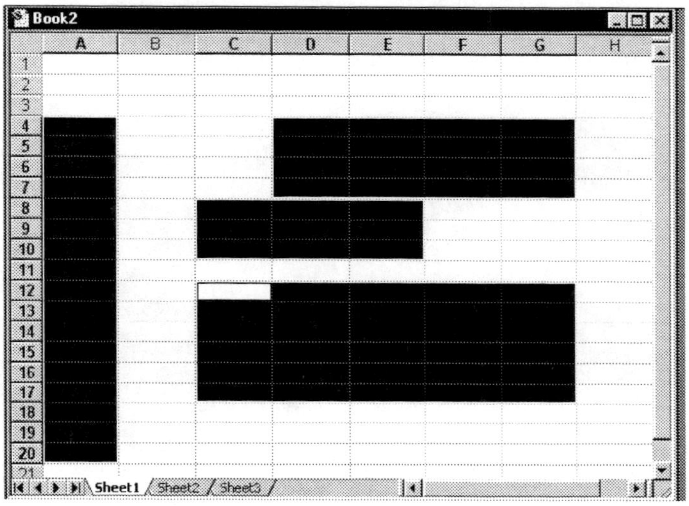

5. Remove the range selections.

6. Select the entire columns C and E as a noncontiguous range. Your worksheet should look like the one shown below:

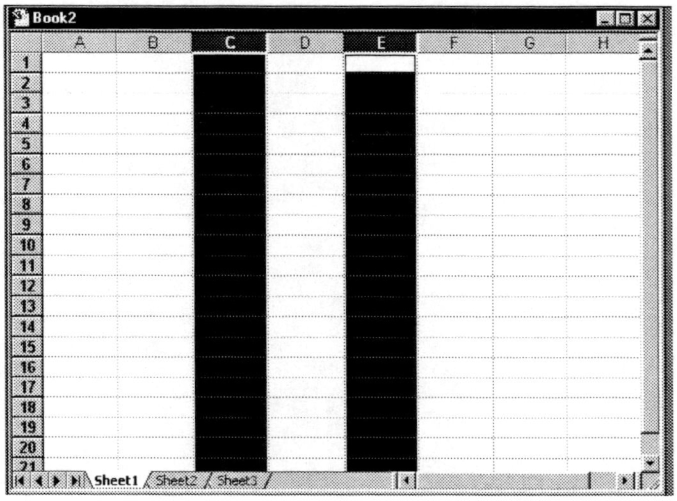

Using Formula Bar Buttons

When you begin to type, three buttons appear to the left of the formula bar: Cancel, Enter, and Edit Formula, as displayed below:

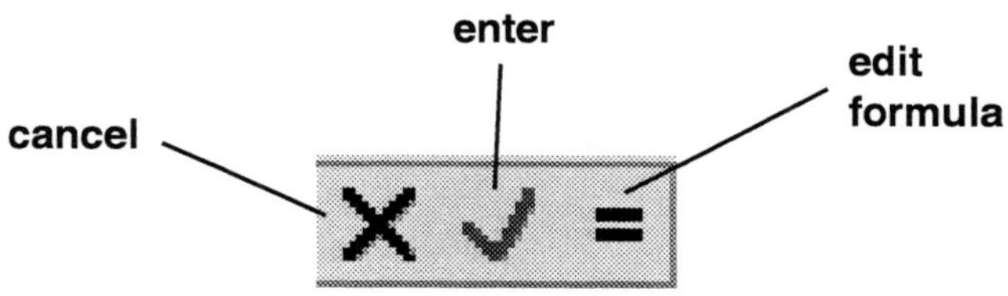

The *Cancel* button can be used to cancel an entry before it is actually entered into the worksheet. Clicking this icon erases anything you have typed, and deactivates the formula bar. It also restores the previous contents of the active cell, if that cell contained another entry. The *Enter* button can be used to complete an entry. Finally, the *Edit Formula* button displays the *Formula Palette*, which provides help when you create formulas that use Excel's built-in functions.

Entering Text

A *text entry*, which is sometimes called a *label*, is one that contains the characters A through Z, or any other character that does not have a purely numeric value. Sometimes a text entry may include numbers, such as in a street address.

By default, a text entry appears left-justified in a cell. If the entry is longer than the defined width of the cell, it either "spills over" into the adjacent cell (if that cell is empty), or appears in truncated form (if the adjacent cell is not empty). Internally, however, it is stored in only one cell and includes all characters originally entered.

Entering Numeric Entries

A *numeric entry* is one that contains the digits 0 through 9 and, optionally, the following special characters:

+	to indicate a positive value
- or ( )	to indicate a negative value
$	to indicate a currency value
%	to indicate a percentage
/	to indicate a fraction
.	to indicate a decimal value
,	to separate the digits of the entry
E or e	to display the entry in scientific (exponential) notation

If you start an entry with a plus sign to indicate a positive number, Excel ignores the sign. If you enter parentheses to indicate a negative number, the program displays the number with a minus sign. If you include a dollar sign, percent sign, forward slash, comma, or exponential symbol, the program automatically assigns a default numeric format to the entry.

By default, a numeric entry appears right-justified in a cell. If the entry is longer than the defined width of the cell, it is either displayed in scientific notation, or it is rounded. Internally, however, it includes all numbers originally entered.

Entering a Range of Data

To enter data in an individual cell, you simply type the data, then press [Enter]. When you have a number of consecutive entries to make, you can select the range first to enter the data more quickly. With pre-selected cells, the cursor moves to the next cell in the selection when you press [Enter].

To enter a range of cells:

- Select the range of cells.
- Type a cell entry, then press [Enter] to move the cursor to the next cell in the selection.
- Continue entering data and pressing [Enter] until the range is filled.

Adjusting Column Width

Although a cell entry can include up to 32,000 characters, the default column width is only 8.43 characters (when the default font, Arial, is selected). While the displayed value of an entry does not affect the value that is stored internally, you can adjust the column width so that entries appear in full and as entered. To do this, you must adjust the column width.

To adjust multiple columns:

- Select at least one cell from each of the desired columns.
- Click Format on the menu bar.
- Select Column on the Format menu.
- Click Width on the Column submenu to display the following dialog box:

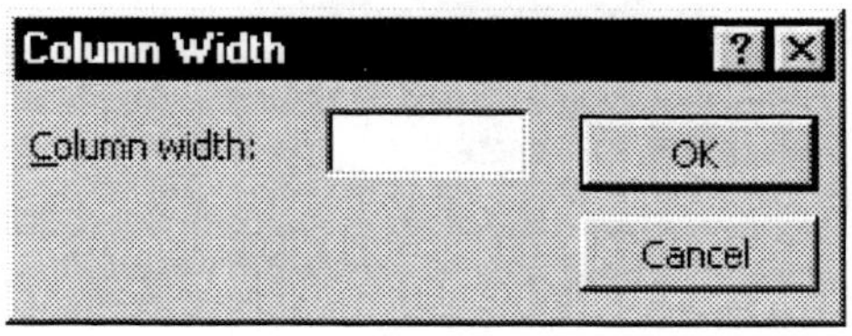

- Type the new width in the Column Width text box.
- Click the OK button.

Two other shortcut methods are possible for adjusting column widths:

- Select the desired columns by highlighting their grey column headers.
- Stretch or shrink all columns by dragging the edge of one of the selected column headers (so that the double-headed arrow appears). All selected columns will be adjusted to that same width.

If you want to quickly adjust column widths to a precise measurement:

- Select the desired columns by highlighting their grey column headers.
- Right-click anywhere in the selected area to display an Object menu.
- Click Column Width.
- Specify a column width, and click OK.

Activating Edit Mode

There are three different methods for activating Edit mode. One method is to select the cell, then click anywhere in the formula bar to activate it. The second method is to double-click the cell to activate Edit mode. The third method is to select the cell, then press [F2] to activate the cell and position the insertion point in the cell. When Edit mode is activated, the mode indicator in the status bar displays the word "Edit."

Editing an Entry

Whether in the formula bar or directly in the cell, you edit an entry by deleting, inserting, or replacing characters.

To delete one or more characters, position the mouse pointer to the left of the character and press [Delete], or to the right of the character and press [Backspace]. To delete multiple characters, select the desired characters, then press [Delete]. You can also delete the entire contents of a cell by clicking in the cell and pressing [Delete].

To insert one or more characters, position the insertion point at the desired location, then type the new data. As data is typed, existing data is moved to the right.

To replace one or more characters, position the insertion point at the desired location, then select the characters to be replaced. Type the new data, then press [Enter]. To simply replace cell contents, select the desired cell, then type the new data and press [Enter]. The new data will replace the existing data.

Naming a File

Like any application running in Windows 95, a *file name* can contain up to 255 characters but cannot include any of the following characters:

* / \ > < ?	: “

Saving a File

You save a file the first time by displaying the Save As dialog box.

To save a file:

- Click File on the menu bar.
- Click Save (or Save As) on the File menu.
- Type a name for the file in the File name text box, then expand the Save in drop-down list box and select a location, if necessary.
- Click the Save button.

Using Mathematical Operators

When you enter a formula into a cell, the calculated result of the formula is displayed, and the formula itself is internally stored. To view the formula, click the cell containing the formula. The formula will display in the formula bar. Each time a reference in a formula is changed, the formula result is changed.

You can use any of the following mathematical operators in a formula:

Operator:	**Meaning:**
^	Exponentiation
*	Multiplication
/	Division
+	Addition
-	Subtraction

When two or more operators are included in a formula, operations are performed according to operator precedence. For example, exponentiation is always performed before any other operation. Multiplication and division are performed next in a left-to-right order, followed by addition and subtraction, again in a left-to-right order.

You can override this precedence by using parentheses, as displayed below:

2 + 4 * 6 / 3 - 1 = 9
(2 + 4) * 6 / 3 - 1 = 11
2 + 4 * (6 / 3 - 1) = 6
(2 + 4) * 6 / (3 - 1) = 18

Building a Formula

Creating a formula is similar to entering text or numbers in that you begin by selecting the cell in which the result of the formula is to appear. To build the formula, you can choose either of the following two methods.

The first method involves inputting the cell references, constant values, and mathematical operators from the keyboard, including any parentheses necessary to change the operator order of priority. You begin by typing an equal sign to activate the formula bar.

The second method involves pointing to cells in the worksheet, and pasting the references for those cells into the formula. Operators and necessary parentheses are still input from the keyboard, as are any constant values. The formula must still begin with an equal sign.

Using AutoSum

You can total a range of cells by manually creating a formula such as A5+B5+C5; however, Excel provides an alternate method, called AutoSum, to manually typing the formula. *AutoSum* automatically totals consecutive values above or to the left of the AutoSum cell.

To automatically total a consecutive range of cells:

- Select the cell that will contain the total.

- Click the AutoSum button on the toolbar to display a formula similar to the following:

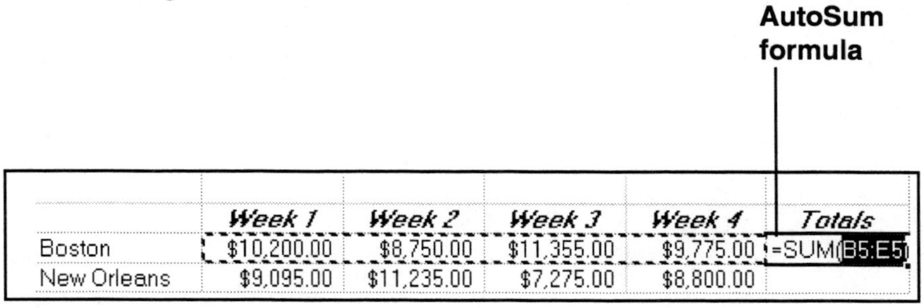

- Modify the range if desired.

- Press [Enter].

Copying a Formula

To copy a formula:

- Select the cell in which the formula appears, and all cells into which the formula is to be copied.
- Click Edit on the menu bar.
- Click Fill on the Edit menu.
- Select Down, Right, Up, or Left to copy the formula into the respective cells.

Using the Fill Handle

To copy a formula using the fill handle:

- Select the cell in which the formula appears, then point to the fill handle.
- Drag the fill handle to the end of the range.

Formatting Numeric Entries

Excel breaks the available numeric formats into categories. The following describes the available categories:

General	has no specific number format.
Number	displays numbers as they are entered.
Currency	displays general monetary values.
Accounting	lines up currency symbols and decimal points.
Date	displays date serial numbers as date values.
Time	displays time serial numbers as time values.
Percentage	multiplies cell values by 100, and displays the result with a percent symbol.
Fraction	displays fractions.
Scientific	uses scientific or exponential notation.
Text	treats values as text.
Special	displays lists and database values such as phone numbers and social security numbers.
Custom	creates custom formats.

Formatting a Range of Cells

To format one or more numeric entries:

- Select the cells to be formatted.
- Click Format on the menu bar.
- Click Cells on the Format menu to display the following dialog box:

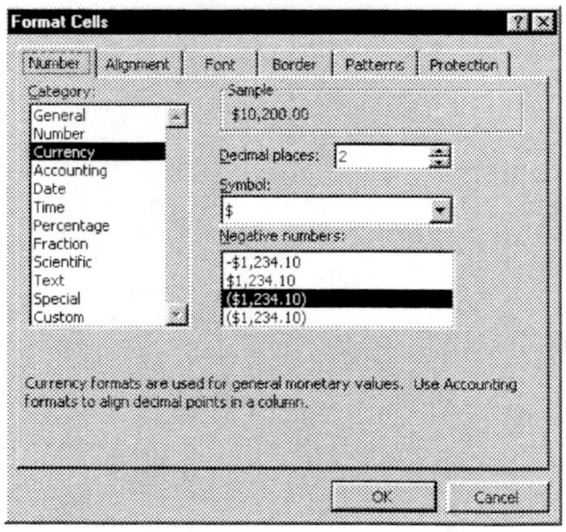

- Select the desired format type in the Category list box.
- Select the desired format in the Type list box, if displayed.
- Click the OK button.

Copying and Moving a Range of Cells

To move a range of cells, select all cells to be moved, then drag the range to the desired starting location. To copy a range, select the range and click Edit on the menu bar, then click Copy. Position the cursor in the starting location for the new range. Click Copy on the menu bar, then click Paste.

Printing a Worksheet

Excel allows you to print selected ranges of data, all the data in a workbook, or simply a single sheet of data. You can select the desired range of cells you want to print prior to displaying the Print dialog box, or you can select the amount you want to print from the Print dialog box.

To print a worksheet:

- Click File on the menu bar.
- Click Print on the File menu.
- Make selections as desired.
- Click the OK button.

Previewing a File

To preview the current sheet:

- Click File on the menu bar.
- Click Print Preview on the File menu.

NOTE: The mouse pointer displays as a magnifying glass when properly positioned in the Preview window.

Closing a Workbook File

To close a workbook file without exiting Excel:

- Click File on the menu bar.
- Click Close on the File menu.

Summary of Lesson 2

Shortcut

To enter a range of cells:

- Select the range of cells.
- Type a cell entry, then press **[Enter]**.
- Continue entering data and pressing **[Enter]** until the range is filled.

To adjust multiple columns:

Shortcut: Select the column headers for the desired colummns, then stretch or shrink by dragging an edge of one of the selected column headers.

- Select at least one cell from each of the desired columns.
- Click **Format** on the menu bar.
- Select **Column** on the Format menu.
- Click **Width** on the Column submenu.
- Type the new width in the Column Width text box.
- Click the **OK** button.

To save a file:

Shortcut: Press **[Ctrl]** + **[F5]** to automatically save a file and bypass the File and Save steps. If a file already has a name, click the **Save** button to bypass these steps.

- Click **File** on the menu bar.
- Click **Save** on the File menu.
- Type a name for the file in the File name text box, then expand the Save in drop-down list box and select a location, if necessary.
- Click the **Save** button.

To automatically total a consecutive range of cells:

- Select the cell that will contain the total.
- Click the **AutoSum** button Σ on the toolbar.
- Modify the range if desired.
- Press **[Enter]**.

To copy a formula:

- Select the cell in which the formula appears, and all cells into which the formula is to be copied.
- Click **Edit** on the menu bar.
- Click **Fill** on the Edit menu.
- Select **Down**, **Right**, **Up**, or **Left** to copy the formula into the respective cells.

Shortcut

To copy a formula using the fill handle:

- Select the cell in which the formula appears, then click the fill handle.
- Drag the fill handle to the end of the range.

To format one or more numeric entries:

Shortcut: **[Ctrl] + [1]**, or double-click in the selected range to display the Object menu, then select **Format Cells**.

- Select the cells to be formatted.
- Click **Format** on the menu bar.
- Click **Cells** on the Format menu.
- Select the desired format type in the Category list box.
- Select the desired format in the Type list box, if displayed.
- Click the **OK** button.

To move a range of cells:

- Select all cells to be moved, then drag the range to the desired starting location.

To copy a range:

Shortcut: **[Ctrl] + [X]** to cut

[Ctrl] + [C] to copy
[Ctrl] + [V] to paste

- Select the range and click **Edit** on the menu bar, then click **Copy**.
- Position the cursor in the starting location for the new range.
- Click **Copy** on the menu bar, then click **Paste**.

To print a selected range in a worksheet:

Shortcut: **[Ctrl] + [P]**

- Click **File** on the menu bar.
- Click **Print** on the File menu.
- Make selections as desired, then click the **OK** button.

To print all pages in the active worksheet:

- Click the **Print** button on the toolbar.

To preview the current sheet:

Shortcut: Click the **Print Preview** button on the toolbar.

- Click **File** on the menu bar.
- Click **Print Preview** on the File menu.

To close a workbook file without exiting Excel:

Shortcut: Click the workbook's **Close** box.

- Click **File** on the menu bar.
- Click **Close** on the File menu.

Practice Exercise A — Lesson 2

1. Display a new, empty workbook file.

2. Create the following worksheet. Increase the width of column A to 16 characters:

	A	B	C	D	E
1		EXPENSES FOR THREE MONTHS			
2					
3		January	February	March	
4	Rent	650	650	650	
5	Utilities	250	250	250	
6	Food	125	100	125	
7	Automobile	375	375	375	
8	Insurance	78.5	68.84	76.5	
9	Clothing	100	50	100	
10	Entertainment	150	125	100	
11					
12	TOTAL				
13					

3. Format all numeric entries as currency with two decimal places.

4. Enter a formula in cell B12 to calculate the total expenses for January. Use only cell references in the formula. Copy the formula into the adjacent columns to calculate the total expenses for February and March.

5. Apply the currency with a two-decimal-place format to the total numeric entries, then increase column width for columns B, C, and D to 9 characters.

6. Change the January insurance entry to 98.50, and the March utilities entry to 195.00. The worksheet should look similar to the following:

	A	B	C	D	E
1		EXPENSES FOR THREE MONTHS			
2					
3		January	February	March	
4	Rent	$650.00	$650.00	$650.00	
5	Utilities	$250.00	$250.00	$195.00	
6	Food	$125.00	$100.00	$125.00	
7	Automobile	$375.00	$375.00	$375.00	
8	Insurance	$98.50	$68.84	$76.50	
9	Clothing	$100.00	$50.00	$100.00	
10	Entertainment	$150.00	$125.00	$100.00	
11					
12	TOTAL	$1,748.50	$1,618.84	$1,621.50	

7. Save the workbook file with the name Work1-2.

8. Print the worksheet, then close the workbook file.

Practice Exercise B — Lesson 2

1. Open the file named Book2.

2. Create a formula in cell F4 to calculate the total Rent for all three months. Copy this formula for all expense categories.

3. In cell F12, create a grand total of expenses for all three months.

4. Create a label called YEARLY TOTAL in cell E13. Resize column E to 12 characters. Then, calculate the yearly total in cell F13 by multiplying the value in cell F12 by 4.

5. Change all numeric entries to Accounting format with no symbol. Your spreadsheet should now look like the one shown below:

	A	B	C	D	E	F
1		EXPENSES FOR THREE MONTHS				
2						
3		January	February	March		TOTAL
4	Rent	650.00	650.00	650.00		1,950.00
5	Utilities	250.00	250.00	195.00		695.00
6	Food	125.00	100.00	125.00		350.00
7	Automobile	375.00	375.00	375.00		1,125.00
8	Insurance	98.50	68.84	76.50		243.84
9	Clothing	100.00	50.00	100.00		250.00
10	Entertainment	150.00	125.00	100.00		375.00
11						
12	TOTAL	1,748.50	1,618.84	1,621.50		4,988.84
13					YEARLY TOTAL	19,955.36

6. Change displayed decimal places to none, so that no decimals are displayed.

7. Print the worksheet, excluding all totals.

8. Close the worksheet without saving it. Close any other open worksheets, but do not close the Excel program.

Practice Exercise C — Lesson 2

1. Open the file called Shoe Company.

2. Create a formula in cell E6 that increases the amount shown in D6 by 30 percent.

3. Create a formula in cell E7 that adds 2,000 to the amount shown in cell D7.

4. In row 10, calculate totals for sales for all four quarters.

5. Move the titles in rows 1 and 2 from column B to column C. Your worksheet should now look like the one shown below:

	A	B	C	D	E
1			National Shoe Company		
2			1997 Sales		
3					
4		1st Quarter	2nd Quarter	3rd Quarter	4th Quarter
5	Running	$45,239.00	$48,956.00	$54,673.00	$42,335.00
6	Tennis	$32,564.00	$28,765.00	$31,776.00	$41,308.80
7	Hiking	$24,567.00	$24,677.00	$25,456.00	$27,456.00
8	Biking	$42,876.00	$44,871.00	$43,671.00	$54,698.00
9					
10	Total	$145,246.00	$147,269.00	$155,576.00	$165,797.80

6. Print columns A and B.

7. Save the worksheet with the same name.

Opening a Workbook

Excel keeps track of the files you have recently opened during the current lesson. To reopen one of these files, you can display the File menu, then click the desired file name at the bottom of the File menu.

To open a workbook file that has not been opened recently:

- Click File on the menu bar.
- Click Open on the File menu to display the Open dialog box.
- Select the file name in the Look in list box *or*

  Type the file name, including an optional drive or directory designation, in the File name text box.
- Click the Open button.

  NOTE: You can also click the Open button on the Standard toolbar to display the Open dialog box.

Changing the View Mode

By default, file names are displayed in the Open dialog box in List view. *List view* simply displays the file name. You can also display files in other view modes, including Details, Properties, and Preview. *Details view* displays the file name, size, type, and the date each file was created or last modified. *Properties view* displays file properties such as the author of the file, the date the file was created, the template the file is using, as well as other file information. *Preview* displays the contents of the file without actually opening the file.

To change view modes, click the appropriate button on the Open dialog box toolbar as displayed below:

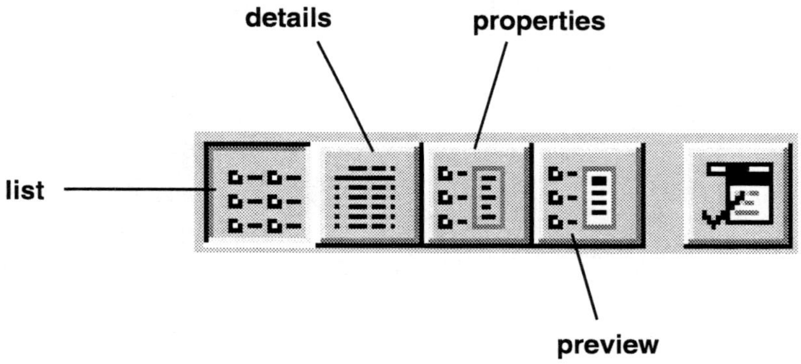

In both Preview and Properties view, the contents and statistics of the selected file are displayed in the right-half of the Look in list box, as displayed below:

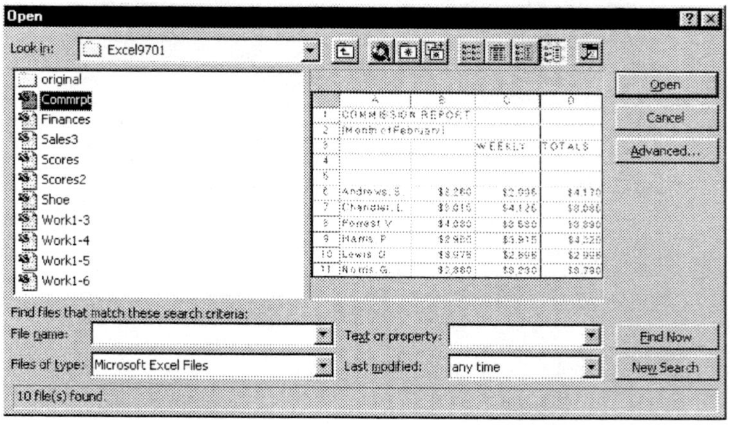

Inserting a Column or Row

When you insert a column or row, Excel shifts existing data horizontally or vertically, as necessary, to create space for the inserted column or row. Formulas that reference a shifted cell are automatically adjusted to reflect the new location of that cell. To insert one or more columns or rows, you select at least one cell in the desired column or row, then click Insert on the menu bar, and click Rows or Columns on the Insert menu, as appropriate.

Deleting a Column or Row

When deleting columns and rows, Excel shifts existing data to close up the extra space. Formulas that reference a deleted cell may result in an error once the column or row is deleted.

To delete a column or row:

- Select at least one cell in the column or row, then click Edit on the menu bar.
- Click Delete on the Edit menu.
- Make a selection as desired.
- Click the OK button.

Clearing Cell Contents

When you delete the contents of a cell or range of cells using [Delete], the values are deleted but the formatting remains intact. To delete contents as well as formatting, you can use the *Clear* command. You can select All from the Clear menu to delete contents and formatting, or select Contents or Format to delete cell contents or cell formatting respectively.

To clear one or more cells using the Clear command:

- Select the desired cells.
- Click Edit on the menu bar.
- Select Clear on the Edit menu.
- Make a selection as desired.

Undoing Operations

You can reverse most deletions using the *Undo* command. The Undo command tracks the last operation you performed, and displays the appropriate undo command when accessed.

To perform an undo operation:

- Click Edit on the menu bar.
- Click Undo on the Edit menu.

You can also undo an operation by clicking the Undo button on the Standard toolbar.

Filling a Range of Cells

To fill a range of cells with dates, months, or other patterns, you begin by displaying the Series dialog box. From the Series dialog box, you can select the fill type and increment, if necessary. Clicking AutoFill fills the selected range with the current pattern.

To fill a range of cells:

- Enter the data pattern, then select the range of cells to be filled, including the data pattern.
- Click Edit on the menu bar.
- Select Fill on the Edit menu.
- Click Series on the Fill submenu to display the following dialog box:

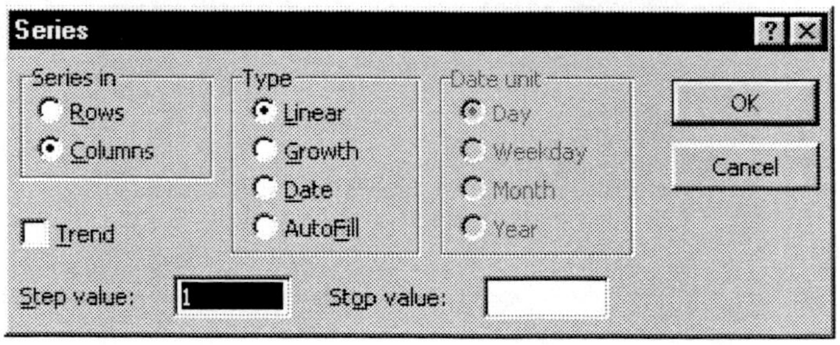

- In the Type section, click AutoFill.
- Click the OK button.

Using the Fill Handle

To quickly fill cells with a continued pattern:

- Type the beginning value in the desired cell.
- Point to the fill handle, then drag to the end of the range.

If the pattern is more complex than a simple increase in numbers by one each cell, you can enter multiple values to define the series pattern, as displayed below:

Value	Fill Pattern
A100	A100
A200	A200
	A300
	A400

Using AutoComplete

The *AutoComplete* command can complete cell entries for you. When you enter repeated data into a range of cells, Excel remembers the data you have entered. Then when you type the first few letters of the desired entry, Excel will complete the entry based on your current list. You can also display a list of the entered data by right-clicking the cell, then choosing Pick from the list.

Creating Absolute Formulas

By default, all formulas when initially created are relative formulas. *Relative referencing* means that the cell addresses in a formula change when the formula is copied to a new location. For example, if cell C1 contains the formula A1*B1, that formula becomes A2*B2 when it is copied into cell C2. A1 and B1 are considered relative addresses because they vary according to the row in which they appear.

Absolute referencing means that the cell address in a formula will not change when the formula is copied. Referring to the above example, if cell A1 contained a constant value on which all formulas in column C depended, that reference should not change from row to row. If the cell references are absolute, when the formula is copied to cell C2, the formula would become A1*B2.

You make a formula absolute by first selecting the formula in the formula bar, then pressing [F4]. The visual indicator that defines an absolute formula is dollar signs ($), which surround the absolute cell reference. You can also manually insert dollar signs within a formula to make the reference absolute. When you use the Fill handle to fill cells with a formula, the Fill will use relative referencing unless you specify that the initial cell formula is to be absolute.

Moving and Copying Cell Entries

As an alternative to using the fill handle on a cell to copy a formula, you can use the Copy and Paste commands. You can access Copy and Paste from the Edit menu, or by displaying an Object menu. To display an Object menu, select the desired cell or range of cells, right-click the selected block, then click the appropriate command as needed.

To copy a range of cells using the Edit menu:

- Select the cell or range of cells, then click Edit on the menu bar.
- Click Copy on the Edit menu.

  NOTE: To move a range of cells, click Cut instead of Copy.

- Select the cell or range of cells to which you want to copy the source block.
- Click Edit on the menu bar, then click Paste on the Edit menu.

You can also copy and move data using the following buttons on the Standard toolbar:

You begin by selecting the desired cell or range of cells, then clicking the Copy or Move button. To paste the data, select the cell or range of cells to which you want to copy the source block. Then click the Paste button.

Realigning Cell Entries

Text entries are normally left-justified in a cell, while numeric entries are normally right-justified. You can change cell alignment to left, right, or center.

To horizontally realign one or more cell entries:

- Select the cell(s) to be aligned, then click Format on the menu bar.
- Click Cells on the Format menu to display the Format Cells dialog box.
- Click the Alignment tab to display the following:

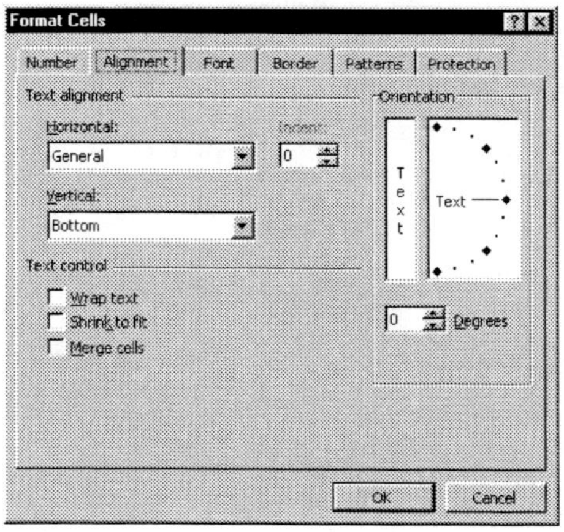

- In the Horizontal section, select the desired alignment. If you want to indent the cell entries (which only makes sense if they are left-aligned to begin with), click the up or down arrow buttons next to the Indent box.
- Click the OK button.

Changing the Font of Cell Entries

To change the font of one or more cell entries:

- Select the cell(s).
- Click Format on the menu bar.
- Click Cells on the Format menu.
- Click the Font tab to display the following:

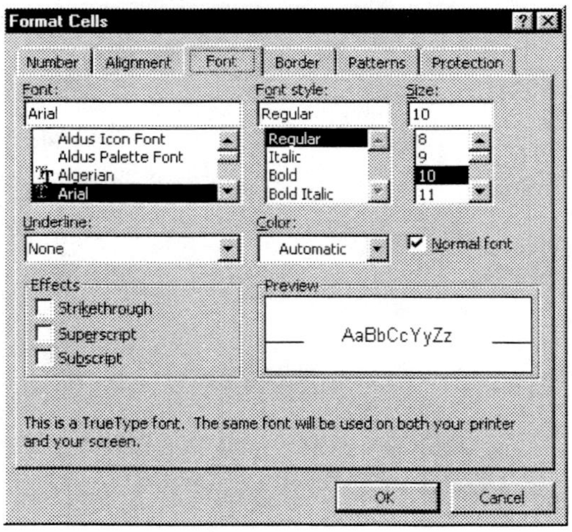

- Select options as desired.
- Click the OK button.

Adding Borders to a Worksheet

To add a border around cells in a worksheet:

- Select the cell(s).
- Click Format on the menu bar.
- Click Cells on the Format menu.
- Click the Border tab to display the following:

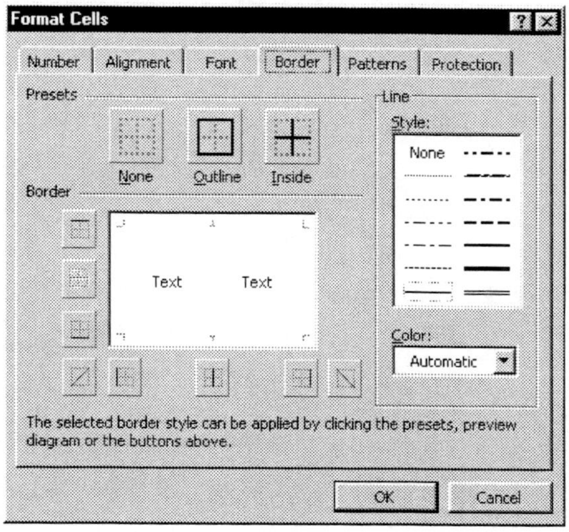

- Select a border in the Presets or the Border section.
- Select a new line style in the Style section, if desired.
- Click the OK button.

A fast way to add borders to selected cells is to click the drop-down arrow next to the Borders button on the toolbar, then select a border from the list of options.

You can also shade cells in a worksheet. You begin by displaying the Patterns section of the Format Cells dialog box, then selecting a shading color from the color palette. You can also choose a pattern if desired.

Using the Toolbar to Perform Formatting Operations

The Formatting toolbar features several formatting buttons that can be used to enhance cell entries. To change formatting characteristics, select the desired cells, then click the appropriate button, as displayed below:

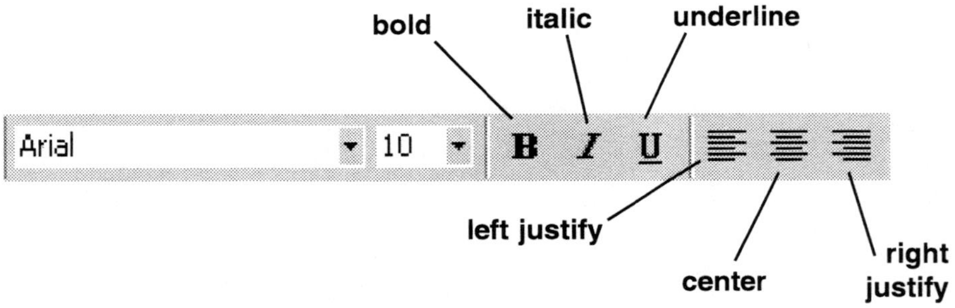

Sorting Data

Excel allows you to sort rows of data in ascending or descending order, either alphabetically or numerically. The sort is based upon a particular column of data. For instance, rows 5 through 10 of a worksheet might contain sales numbers for various cities. The name of each city would appear as a label in column A. So, it might make sense to select rows 5 through 10 for sorting and specify column A as the column on which to base the sort.

To sort data in a worksheet:

- Select the range that you want to sort, then click Data on the menu bar.
- Click Sort to display the Sort dialog box.
- Select the column to sort by (column A is the default), then click OK.

You can also sort on multiple levels of a worksheet. However, this task is not required for the proficiency test. In most cases, you will want to sort by rows—that is, from the top row of the selection to the bottom row of the selection. However, there may be situations where you want to sort the selection by columns—that is, from left to right.

To sort by columns:

- Select the range that you want to sort, then click Data on the menu bar.
- Click Sort to display the Sort dialog box, then click the Options button.
- Click the Sort left to right option button, then click the OK button.

Summary of Lesson 3

Shortcut

To open a workbook file:

Shortcut: Click the **Open** icon on the toolbar.

To open a recently used file, click the **Start** button and select the file from the list.

- Click **File** on the menu bar.
- Click **Open** on the File menu.
- Select the file name in the Look in list box *or*
  Type the file name, including an optional drive or directory designation, in the File name text box.
- Click the **Open** button.

To delete a column or row:

Shortcut: Click the grey row or column header.

- Select at least one cell in the column or row.
- Click **Edit** on the menu bar.
- Click **Delete** on the Edit menu.
- Make a selection as desired.
- Click the **OK** button.

To clear one or more cells using the Clear command:

Shortcut: **[Ctrl] + [Delete]** *or* Right-click the mouse and select **Clear Contents**.

- Select the desired cells.
- Click **Edit** on the menu bar.
- Select **Clear** on the Edit menu.
- Make a selection as desired.

To perform an undo operation:

Shortcut: **[Ctrl] + [Z]**

- Click **Edit** on the menu bar.
- Click **Undo** on the Edit menu.

To fill a range of cells:

Shortcut: Drag the fill handle to see if AutoFill correctly guesses the series.

- Enter the start data, then select the range of cells to be filled, including the start data.
- Click **Edit** on the menu bar.
- Select **Fill** on the Edit menu.
- Click **Series** on the Fill submenu.
- In the Type section, click **AutoFill**.
- Click the **OK** button.

<u>**Shortcut**</u>	**To quickly fill cells with a continued pattern:**
	• Type the beginning value in the desired cell. • Point to the fill handle, then drag to the end of the range.
	To copy a range of cells:
[Ctrl] + [C] *or* Right-click the selection and select **Copy**. **[Ctrl] + [V]** *or* Right-click the selection and select **Paste**.	• Select the cell or range of cells. • Click **Edit** on the menu bar. • Click **Copy** on the Edit menu. • Select the cell or range of cells to which you want to copy the source block. • Click **Edit** on the menu bar. • Click **Paste** on the Edit menu.
	To horizontally realign one or more cell entries:
[Ctrl] + [1] *or* Click one of the Alignment buttons for left, center, or right alignment. Use the **Decrease Indent** and **Increase Indent** buttons to indent cell content incrementally. Use the **Merge and Center** button to center cell contents across a selection.	• Select the cell(s) to be aligned. • Click **Format** on the menu bar. • Click **Cells** on the Format menu. • Click the **Alignment** tab. • In the Horizontal section, select the desired alignment or indentation. • Click the **OK** button.
	To change the font of one or more cell entries:
Click the Font drop-down list on the toolbar and select a font.	• Select the cell(s). • Click **Format** on the menu bar. • Click **Cells** on the Format menu. • Click the **Font** tab. • Select options as desired. • Click the **OK** button.

Shortcut

Click the Borders drop-down list on the toolbar and select a border option.

To add a border to a worksheet:

- Select the cell(s).
- Click **Format** on the menu bar.
- Click **Cells** on the Format menu.
- Click the **Border** tab.
- Select a border in the Border section.
- Select a new line style in the Style section, if desired.
- Click the **OK** button.

To sort data in a worksheet:

- Select the range that you want to sort, then click Data on the menu bar.
- Click Sort to display the Sort dialog box.
- Select the column to sort by (column A is the default), then click OK.

To sort by columns:

- Select the range that you want to sort, then click Data on the menu bar.
- Click Sort to display the Sort dialog box.
- Click the Options button.
- Click the Sort left to right option button, then click the OK button.

Practice Exercise A — Lesson 3

1. Open the file named Commissions.

2. Sort rows 7 through 14 alphabetically based on column A.

3. Insert a row between rows 8 and 9, then enter the following information in the new row:

Evans, P.	4150	2295	4030	3445

4. Copy the formula in cell F8 to cell F9.

5. Clear the contents of the range A13:E13, retaining formatting, then enter the following information into the range just cleared:

Martin, J.	3890	3120	2895	4115

6. Create a commission formula in cell G7 that multiplies the total sales by the commission rate in cell A20.

   NOTE: Be sure to make the commission reference absolute.

7. Copy the formula to the range G8:G15.

8. Bold the labels in cells A7:A15, then widen column A to 12 characters.

9. Shade the commission values, then place an outline border around the weekly sales values. The worksheet should look similar to the following:

	COMMISSION REPORT (Month of February)					
	WEEKLY TOTALS					
	2/1 - 2/7	2/8 - 2/14	2/15 - 2/21	2/22 - 2/28	Total	Commission
Appleton, S.	$3,260	$2,995	$4,170	$3,580	$14,005	$700.25
Chandler, L.	$3,015	$4,125	$3,085	$2,790	$13,015	$650.75
Evans, P.	$4,150	$2,295	$4,030	$3,445	$13,920	$696.00
Frank, V.	$4,030	$3,580	$3,390	$3,995	$14,995	$749.75
Homes, P.	$2,980	$3,915	$4,320	$3,870	$15,085	$754.25
Lunt, D.	$3,975	$2,895	$2,995	$4,160	$14,025	$701.25
Martin, J.	$3,890	$3,120	$2,895	$4,115	$14,020	$701.00
Robbins, J.	$2,745	$4,080	$2,900	$3,755	$13,480	$674.00
Torres, M.	$3,655	$4,785	$2,875	$4,060	$15,375	$768.75

10. Save and print the workbook file, then clear the workbook window.

Practice Exercise B — Lesson 3

1. Open the file named Weekly Sales.

2. Move the titles in cells A1 and A2 to cells C1 and C2, and then center the text across the selection.

3. Create a label in cell B4 called Week 1. Use the fill series command to create labels for Week 2, Week 3, and Week 4 in cells C4, D4, and E4.

4. Bold and Italicize all labels in row 4.

5. Indent the label in cell A9 three characters to the right.

6. Create a double-line outline border around cells B9 through F9. **HINT:** You will need to use the border selection area in the Format Cells dialog box to specify which edges will receive the border. Your worksheet should look like the one shown below:

		Weekly Sales Totals			
		for 4 Regional Offices			
	Week 1	***Week 2***	***Week 3***	***Week 4***	***Totals***
Boston	$10,200.00	$8,750.00	$11,355.00	$9,775.00	$40,080.00
New Orleans	$9,095.00	$11,235.00	$7,275.00	$8,800.00	$36,405.00
Chicago	$12,115.00	$13,200.00	$9,450.00	$10,235.00	$45,000.00
Phoenix	$6,765.00	$9,885.00	$8,600.00	$11,320.00	$36,570.00
Totals	$38,175.00	$43,070.00	$36,680.00	$40,130.00	$158,055.00

7. Save and close the file.

Practice Exercise C — Lesson 3

1. Open the file Exam Scores.

2. Move the title line from column A to column B on the same row, and change the font size to 14 point.

3. Boldface all column headings.

4. Use the Fill Series command to fill cells A6:A14 with ID numbers, incrementing each ID number by 5 (92-100, 92-105, etc.).

5. Use the fill handle to copy the relative formula in cell F5 to create total scores for all applicants.

6. Center all test scores within their cells.

7. Delete the Humanities column.

8. In the status column, fill all "Fail" cells with the color red (the first color on the third row of the color palette). Your worksheet should look like the one shown below:

9. Save and close the file.

	Entrance Examination Scores				
Applicant ID No.	**Science**	**Math**	**History**	**Total Score**	**Status**
92-100	86	79	85	250	Pass
92-105	69	90	91	250	
92-110	92	93	78	263	Pass
92-115	84	89	79	252	Pass
92-120	87	74	68	229	
92-125	79	77	94	250	Pass
92-130	91	84	75	250	Pass
92-135	90	92	81	263	Pass
92-140	85	76	83	244	
92-145	78	81	94	253	Pass

Creating a Chart

Charts can appear one of two ways: as embedded charts, or as separate sheets in a workbook file. *Embedded charts* appear on the worksheet page and can be viewed and edited directly on the page. *Chart sheets* can be edited when the sheet window is activated.

To create a chart:

- Select the data to be plotted, then click Insert on the menu bar. Select Chart on the Insert menu to display the first Chart Wizard dialog box:

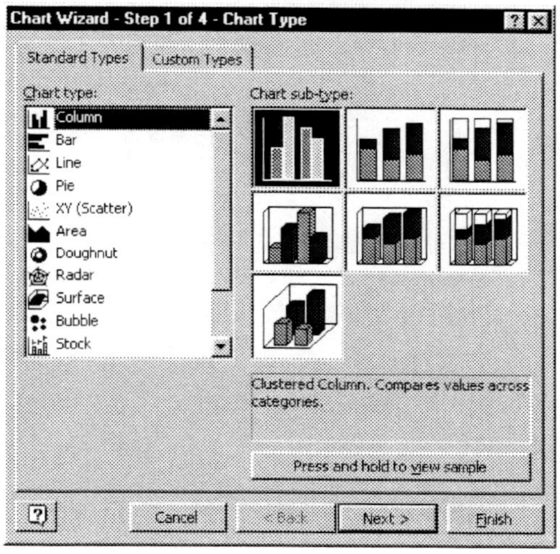

- In dialog box 1, select the chart type, then click the Next> button.
- In the dialog box, enter a title for the chart. Then click the Next> button.
- Click As new sheet to create a chart sheet, or As object in to create an embedded chart. Then click the Finish button.

You can also create an empty chart sheet by pressing [F11]. You can then copy or paste an existing chart into the new sheet. If you press [Alt] + [F1] from a worksheet, Excel will create a chart using the default chart options.

Moving, Resizing, and Deleting a Chart

To move or size a chart, you begin by selecting the chart. When a chart is selected, sizing handles appear around it, as shown below:

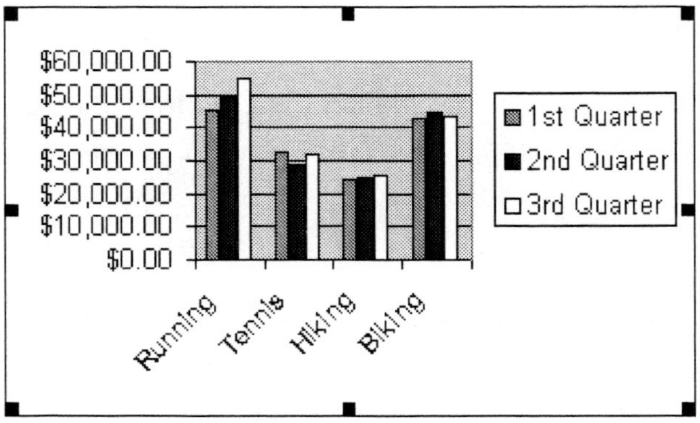

To move a chart, position the mouse pointer over the selected chart and drag to the desired location. To resize a chart, position the mouse pointer over the desired sizing handle, then drag in the appropriate direction. To delete an embedded chart, select the chart, then press [Delete].

Chart Types

The following describes the various chart types from which you can choose:

Area	values are represented by shaded areas.
Bar	values are represented by horizontal bars.
Column	values are represented by vertical bars.
Doughnut	values are represented by sections of a round circle.
Line	values are represented by points. These points may or may not be connected by a line.
Pie	values are represented by wedges of a pie; limited to one data series.

Radar	values are represented by points that radiate from a center point.
XY	ordered pairs of values are represented by horizontal and vertical coordinates.
Surface	shows a 3-D surface representing the relation between two sets of data.
Bubble	an XY chart in which ordered triplets of values are represented by horizontal (X) and vertical (Y) coordinates, as well as by the size of the "bubble" at the coordinates.
Stock	a type of hi-lo-close chart that is often used to show stock prices.
Cone, cylinder, and pyramid	add dramatic visual effects to 3-D column and bar charts.

Additional chart types are available by clicking the Custom Types folder tab in the Chart Wizard.

Changing the Chart Type

To change the chart type:

- Right-click the chart to display the Object menu.
- Click Chart Type on the Object menu to display the chart type dialog box.
- Select the chart type you want.
- Select the desired chart sub-type.

  NOTE: In the dialog box, you can see a chart preview by using the button labeled "Press and hold to view sample." To see the preview, click the button and hold down the mouse button.

- Click the OK button.

Modifying Chart Titles

To modify a chart title:

- Select the chart, then select the chart title.
- If you wish, type new text for the title, then press [Enter].
- Right-click the title to display its object menu. Then select Format Chart Title to display the Format Chart Title dialog box.
- Click the Font tab to display the following:

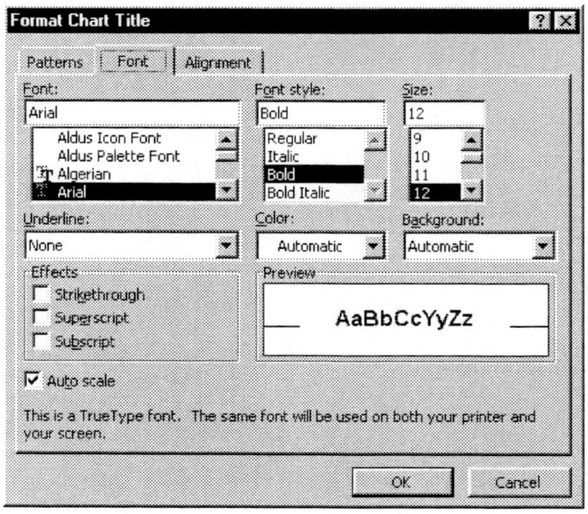

- Make changes as desired.
- Click the OK button.

Adding Borders and Shading

To add a border to the chart title:

- Select the chart, then select the title.
- Right-click the title to display its Object menu.
- Click Format Chart Title.
- Click the Patterns tab to display the following:

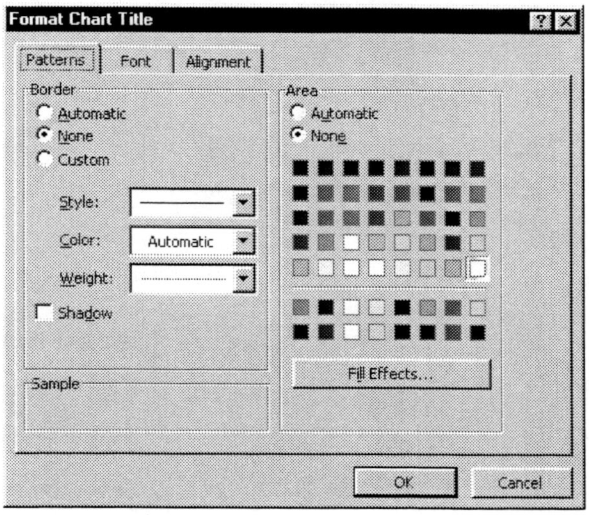

- In the Border section, select the desired border.
- In the Area section, select a border color.
- Click the OK button.

Repositioning a Data Element

New in Excel 97 is the ability to select individual data elements in a chart and drag them with the mouse. Depending on the chart type, some data elements can be moved but others can't. In a pie chart, for example, it's easy to move individual pie slices to explode or un-explode the pie chart. Similar methods work with other types of charts.

To reposition a slice in a pie chart:

- Click the pie itself, then click the slice you want to reposition. A border appears around the slice, indicating that it is selected.
- With the mouse pointer over the slice, hold down the left mouse button and drag the slice out of the pie.

Modifying Other Chart Options

You can change many of the components of the chart after you have created it. To display the Chart Options dialog box:

- Click Chart on the menu bar.
- Click Chart Options in the Chart menu to display the following:

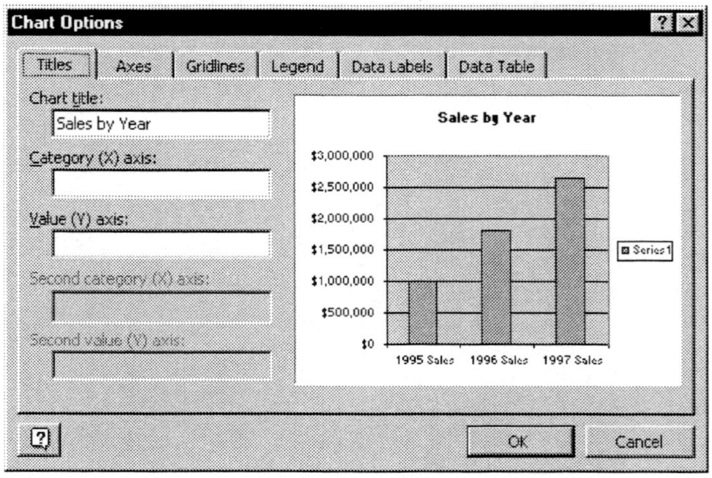

The chart option contains six folder tabs, each of which displays a separate dialog box:

Titles — Allows you to add or change the main chart title, the category axis title, and the value axis title.

Axes — Allows you to remove the category and/or value axis labels. You can also use this dialog box to change the primary axis to become the category axis (often the same as the automatic setting) or as a time scale by date.

Gridlines — Allows you to specify major and/or minor gridlines for both the category and value axes. If you specify minor gridlines for an axis, Excel will display gridlines in small increments.

Legend — Allows you to change the location of the legend.

Data Labels — Allows you to add a value label to each item on the category axis or to add category labels next to each item on the category axis.

Data Table — Adds a table below the chart. The table contains cell values that are used in the chart.

You can also change chart options by double-clicking directly the component within the chart. You have already seen this technique used in changing chart titles. As another example, to change the placement of a chart legend, you can double-click the legend to display a Format Legend dialog box. Then click the Placement tab to display the options shown below:

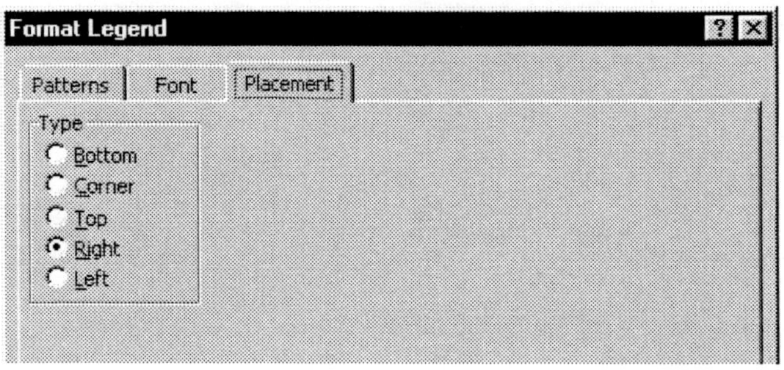

Changing the Page Layout

To change the layout of a chart before printing it, you begin by displaying the Page Setup dialog box. When a chart is activated, the Page Setup dialog box includes an extra tab called Chart, which allows you to control the size of the printed chart.

To modify page layout:

- Select the chart.
- Click File on the menu bar.
- Click Page Setup on the File menu to display the following dialog box:

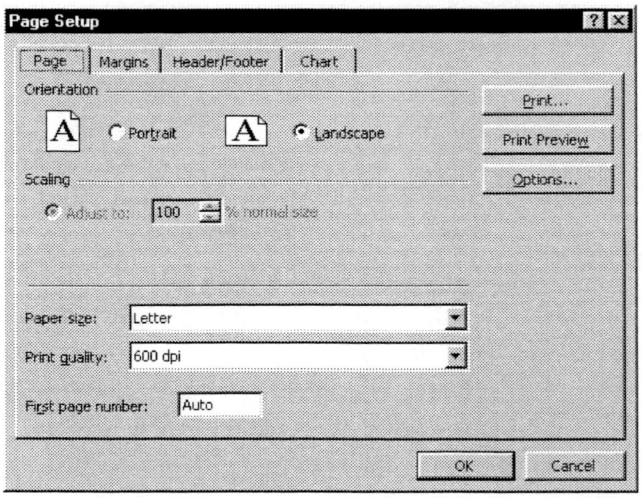

- Make changes as desired.
- Click the OK button.

Modifying the Header and Footer

You can modify the default header or footer of a worksheet by first displaying the Header/Footer section of the Page Setup dialog box, then selecting a built-in header or footer. You can also create a customized header or footer by typing the desired text in the Left, Center, or Right Section edit box.

Previewing the Chart

To preview, then print a chart:

- Select the chart.
- Click File on the menu bar.
- Click Print Preview on the File menu.
- Click the Print button on the Preview toolbar.

Adding and Deleting Sheets

When you add a new sheet to the workbook file, the sheet is inserted before the current sheet. To insert a new sheet, click Worksheet on the Insert menu. To delete a sheet, you must first make that sheet the current sheet.

To delete a sheet:

- Click the desired sheet tab, then click Edit on the menu bar.
- Click Delete Sheet on the Edit menu, then click the OK button.

Naming Sheets

By default, the sheets in a workbook are labeled Sheet1, Sheet2, and so on. You can change the sheet names to make them more descriptive.

To name a sheet:

- Double-click the Sheet tab to highlight the current sheet name.
- Type a new name to replace the old one.
- Press [Enter].

Summary of Lesson 4

Shortcut

To create a chart:

Click the **Chart Wizard** button.
You can elect to skip steps 2, 3, and/or 4 of the Chart Wizard and modify chart elements later. Press **[Alt] + [F1]** to instruct Excel to create a default chart automatically.

- Select the data to be plotted, then click **Insert** on the menu bar.
- Select **Chart** on the Insert menu.
- In dialog box 1, select the chart type, then click the **Next>** button.
- In the dialog box, select the range of data that the chart should display. Then click the **Next>** button.
- In the dialog box, enter a title for the chart. If needed, enter captions for the X and Y axes, data labels, and other chart information. Then click the **Next>** button.
- Click **As new sheet** to create a chart sheet, or **As object in** to create an embedded chart.
- Click the **Finish** button.

To change the chart type:

- Right-click the chart.
- Click **Chart Type** on the Object menu.
- Select the chart type and sub-type.
- Click the **OK** button.

To change a chart title:

If you forget to create a title, select the chart, click **Chart** on the menu bar, then select **Chart options**. Use the Title tab to create a title.

- Click the chart title to select it.
- Type the new title.
- Press **[Enter]**.

To add a border to the chart title:

Double-click the title selection border to automatically display the Format Chart Title dialog box.

- Right-click the chart title to display its Object menu.
- Click **Format Chart Title** on the Object menu.
- Click the **Patterns** tab.
- In the Border section, select the desired border.
- In the Area section, select a border color.
- Click the **OK** button.

Shortcut

To reposition a data element:

- Click the chart, then click the element you want to reposition.
- Drag the element to its new position and release the mouse button.

To modify chart options:

Right-click the chart, then select **Chart options**.

- Select the chart.
- Click **Chart** on the menu bar.
- Click **Chart Options** on the menu bar.
- Click the folder tab for the chart component that you want to modify.
- Change options as desired, then click the **OK** button.

To modify page layout:

- Select the chart.
- Click **File** on the menu bar.
- Click **Page Setup** on the File menu.
- Make changes as desired, then click the **OK** button.

To preview, then print a chart:

Click the **Print Preview** button on the toolbar.

- Select the chart.
- Click **File** on the menu bar.
- Click **Print Preview** on the File menu.
- Click the **Print** button on the Preview toolbar.

To insert a sheet:

Press **[Shift] + [F11]** to insert a new worksheet.

- Click **Insert** on the menu bar, then click **Worksheet**.

To delete a sheet:

- Click the desired sheet tab, then click **Edit** on the menu bar.
- Click **Delete Sheet** on the Edit menu, then click **OK**.

To name a sheet:

- Double-click the **Sheet** tab to highlight the current sheet name.
- Type a new name to replace the old one, then press **[Enter]**.

Practice Exercise A — Lesson 4

1. Open the worksheet named Work1-4.

2. Plot an embedded chart representing the weekly sales totals for New Orleans, Chicago, and Phoenix.

3. Redisplay the chart in a 3-D bar-type format using any subtype desired.

4. Move the legend to the bottom of the chart, then add the following two-line title to the chart:

Weekly Sales Totals 3 Regional Offices

5. Change the font style to one of your choosing, then resize the chart as needed so that the chart looks similar to the following:

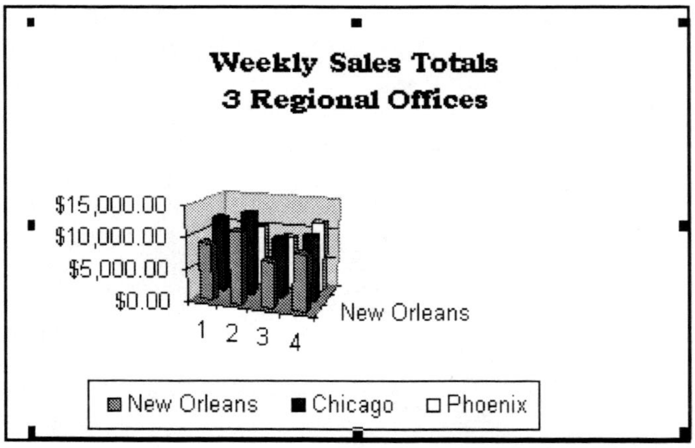

6. Preview, then print the chart.

7. Save, then close the workbook file.

Practice Exercise B — Lesson 4

1. Open the file named Exam Scores.

2. Create a clustered column chart (3-D) for all five scoring categories. Use the ID numbers as the category axis and category axis labels. Use the scores as the values and value labels. Create a chart title that reads Exam Scores. Create the chart in a separate sheet. Your screen should look similar to the following:

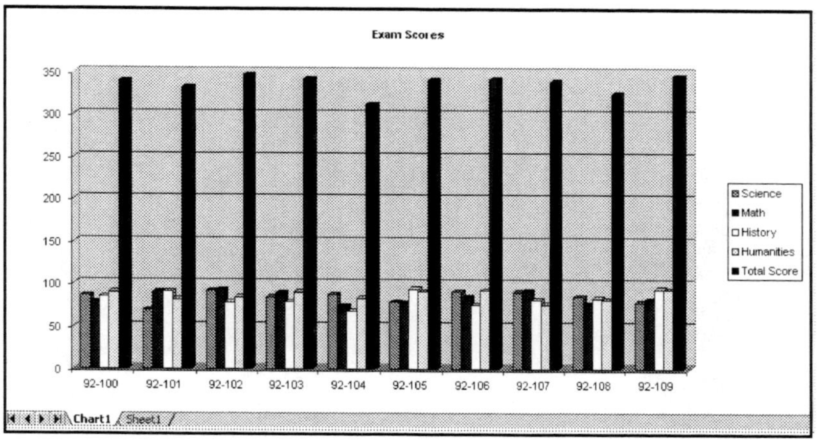

3. Add minor gridlines to the value axis, and display a data table with the chart. Change the title font to 14 point. To improve screen visibility, view the chart so that is sized with the window. Your chart sheet should now look similar to the following:

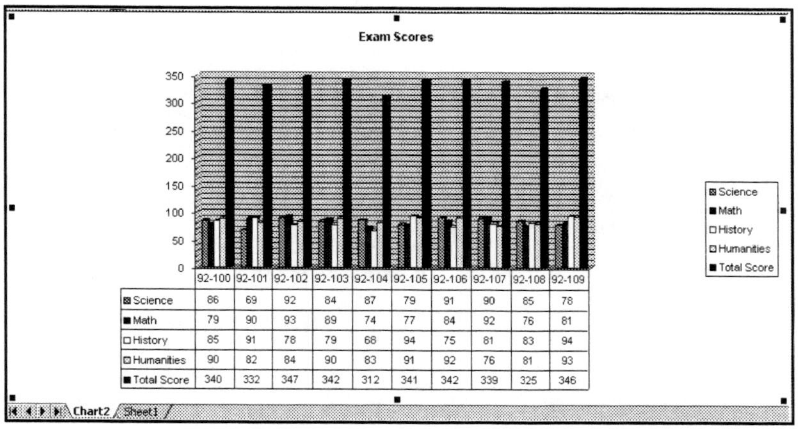

4. Save and close the file.

Practice Exercise C — Lesson 4

1. Open the file named "More Scores."

2. Create a column, cylindrical chart that uses the total score as the value axis, and the ID number as the category axis. *Only chart the Total Score column.* Create data labels for all values. The title of the chart is "Total Score." Embed the chart in the current sheet.

3. Select all data labels for column values, and change the font size to 14. Change the font size of the title to 16 pt., bold.

4. Move all data labels upward so that they do not conflict with the columns or any gridlines. Delete the legend.

5. Create a new chart sheet, then cut and paste the chart into the new sheet. Your final chart should look similar to this one:

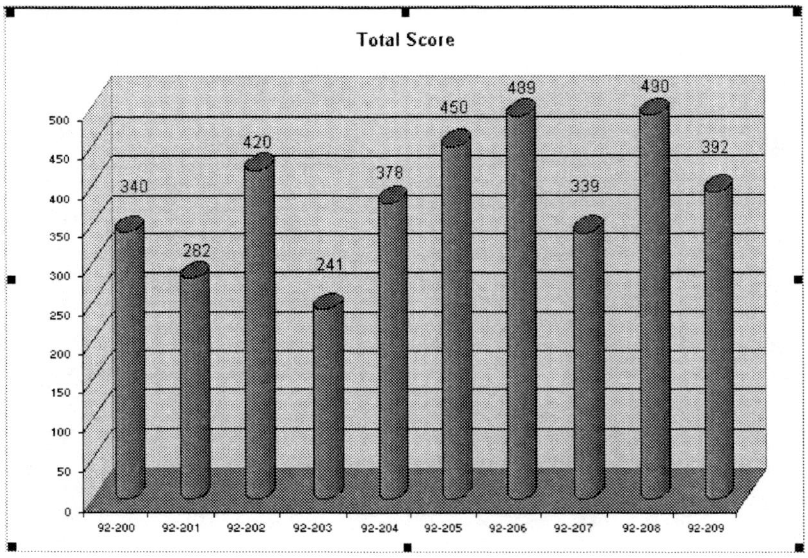

6. Preview, then print the chart sheet.

7. Delete the chart sheet, then close the file without saving changes.

Displaying the Drawing Toolbar

The *Drawing* toolbar contains many buttons and tools that can be used to create various objects in the workbook window. You display the Drawing toolbar by first displaying the Toolbars submenu, then selecting Drawing.

Some of the drawing buttons are as follows:

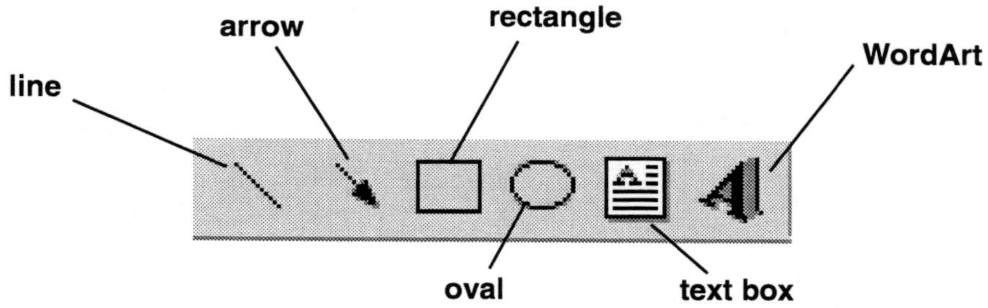

The Drawing toolbar's AutoShapes button displays a menu of predefined shapes you can use instead of plain lines and rectangles.

Creating Basic Shapes

To select an AutoShape:

- Display the Drawing toolbar.
- Click AutoShapes.
- Select a category, then click a shape.
- When the crosshair pointer appears, click and drag to size the shape at the location you want it in your worksheet.

You can move an object easily by clicking the object and dragging it to a new location. You can also resize the object at any time by clicking one of the sizing handles around the edges of the object, then dragging until the object is resized appropriately.

Using Fill Features

If you want to place an object around cells that contain exiting text or values, you need to specify a No Fill for the object; otherwise, the fill color will obscure the content of the cells. However, you can also draw an object over existing text and then re-enter the text directly into the object.

To specify No Fill for an object:

- Click the object until the sizing handles appear.
- Click Format on the menu bar.
- Click AutoShape in the Format menu to display the Format AutoShape dialog box.
- Make sure the Colors and Lines folder tab is selected.
- Click the Fill Color drop-down list box.
- Click the No Fill button at the top of the Colors box.
- Click the OK button.

Adding a Fill Color

You can add colors, shadows, or even 3-D effects to enhance the appearance of the shape. To add a fill color, simply follow the procedures provided above, except select a fill color in the Colors box.

Adding a Shadow to an Object

To add a shadow:

- Select the object so that the size handles appear.
- Display the Drawing toolbar if necessary, then click the Shadow button near the right end of the toolbar to display the following shadow choices:

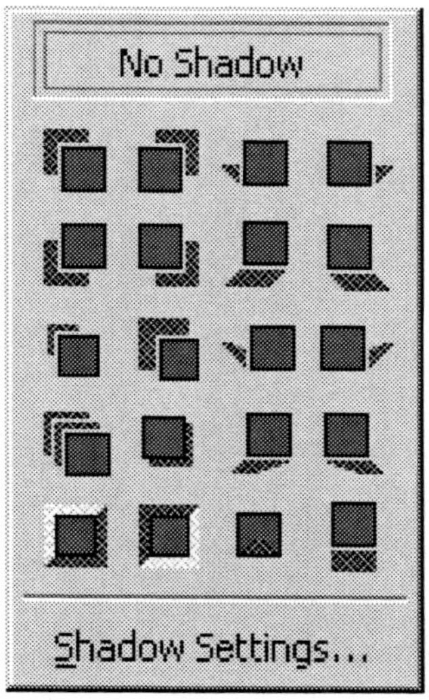

- Select a shadow.

You can use this same procedure to change the shadow effect at any time. To remove a shadow, select the No Shadow button near the top of the shadow choices box. You can also "nudge" a shadow up, down, left, or right by clicking the Shadow Settings button and then clicking one of the nudge buttons.

Adding a 3-D Effect to an Object

To create a 3-D effect, follow the same procedures for creating a shadow, but select the 3-D button in the Drawing toolbar (at the right end, next to the Shadow button).

Other AutoShapes

The following additional AutoShape categories are available:

Lines	Use these AutoShapes to create straight lines, with or without arrowheads, or to create curved, freeform, and squiggly lines. After you create a line from one point in your worksheet to another, you can drag the handles (at either end) upward, downward, in, or out to change the position of the line or to shrink or extend the line.
Connectors	The first three connectors are identical in function to the first three lines in the Lines category. The second row of connectors allow you to create straight lines at right angles, with or without arrows. The third row of connectors allows you to create curved lines, with or without arrows.
Block arrows	This category includes decorative arrows that you can add to your worksheet to call attention to a cell, row, or column.
Flowchart	This category allows you to include flowchart symbols directly into your worksheet. As is true for the Basic Shapes, you can add text directly into a flowchart symbol. By combining flowchart symbols with arrowhead lines or connectors, you can construct true flowcharts.
Stars and Banners	Use the shapes in this category to add decorative bursts, stars, and banners to selected areas of your worksheet. You can enter text directly into these shapes, all some of the shapes do not lend themselves well to text.
Callouts	This category includes balloon shapes, much like you would see in a comic strip. You can enter text directly into any of these shapes.

Inserting a Picture

To insert a picture, simply click Insert on the menu bar, then select Picture. If you want to insert a picture that exists as a file on your hard disk, click From file and locate the file. If you want to insert a Clip Art image, click Clip Art and select the image that you want to insert.

Rotating Text and Graphics

Excel enables you to rotate text in cells as well as graphics. You can rotate a graphic that you have placed or an object (shape) that you have created using the Drawing toolbar.

To rotate the contents of a cell:

- Right-click the cell whose contents you want to indent. This displays the Object menu for the cell.
- In the Object menu, select Format Cells to display the Format Cells dialog box.
- In the dialog box, click the Alignment tab to display the Alignment page of the dialog box.

  NOTE: The Orientation area of the dialog box has a control that looks like the face of a clock. By clicking a point of the clock, you tell Excel how much to rotate the cell contents.

- In the clock face, click the point for the amount of rotation you want to apply to the cell contents.
- Click the OK button.

Creating Headers and Footers

To enter a header or a footer:

- Click File on the menu bar.
- Click Page Setup on the File menu to display the Page Setup dialog box.
- Click the Header/Footer tab to display the following:

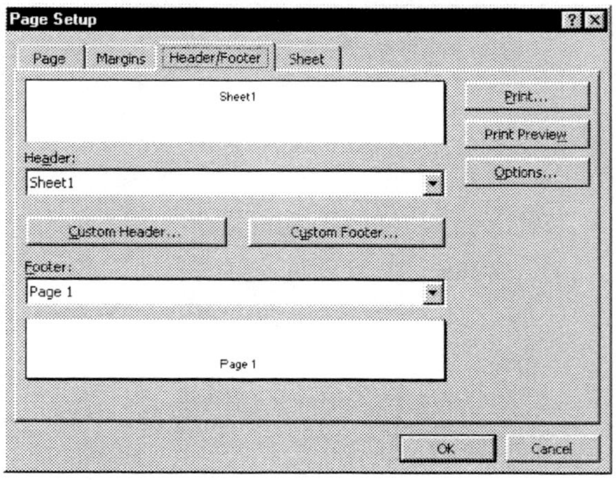

- Expand the Header drop-down list box, then select the desired option.
- Expand the Footer drop-down list box, then select the desired option.
- Click the OK button.

Inserting Codes into Header and Footer Text

You can create a customized header or footer by first clicking the Custom Header or Custom Footer button to display the following:

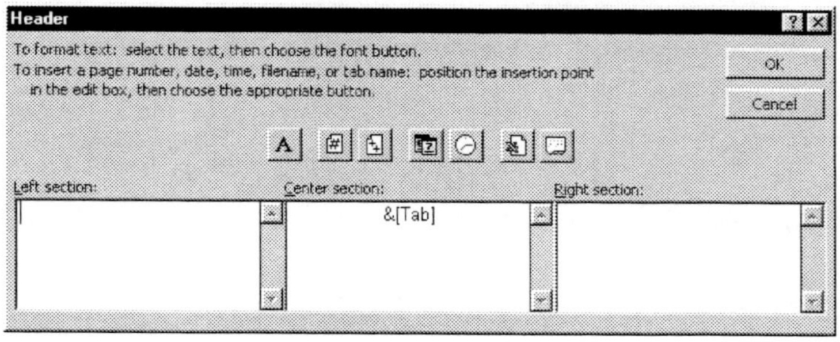

You then click in the desired edit box to specify text alignment, and type the desired text. You can also insert page number, date, time, or file name codes by clicking the appropriate button in the Header/Footer dialog box. You can also modify the font style and the size of text by selecting the text, then clicking the Font button, and making selections as desired.

Page Layout Default Settings

By default, a worksheet will print on 8.5 × 11-inch paper in portrait orientation with the following margins:

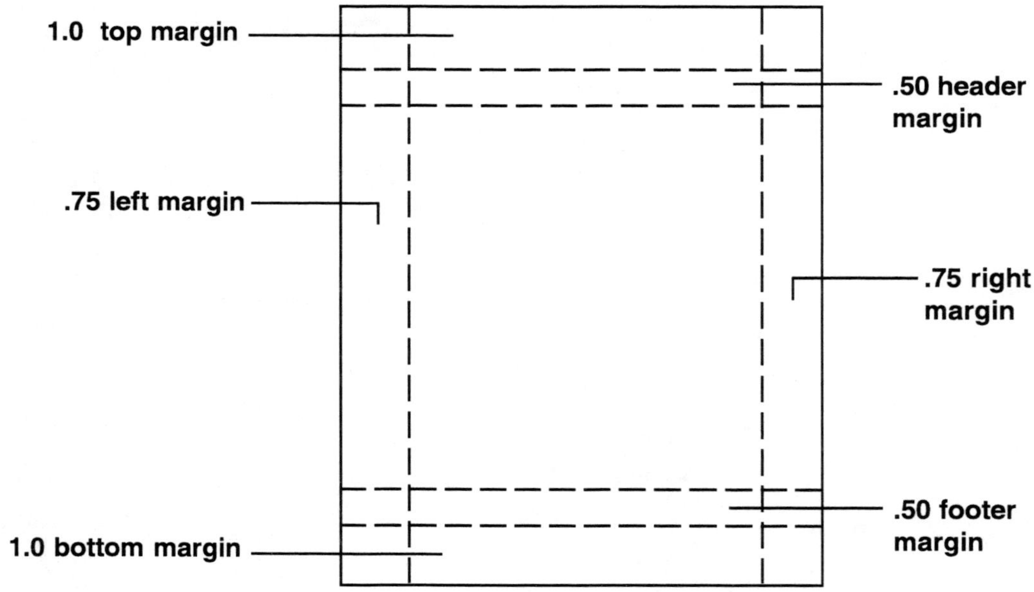

If a header or footer is added to the worksheet, Excel separates the header and footer text from the worksheet by .5 inch. You can view and change left, right, top, and bottom margins, as well as header and footer margins, by displaying the worksheet in the Preview window and activating margin lines.

You can also modify the page layout by adding hard page breaks to a worksheet to paginate the page differently than the default paper type setting dictates.

Changing Margins

To change margin settings from the Page Setup dialog box:

- Click File on the menu bar.
- Click Page Setup on the File menu.
- Click the Margins tab to display the following:

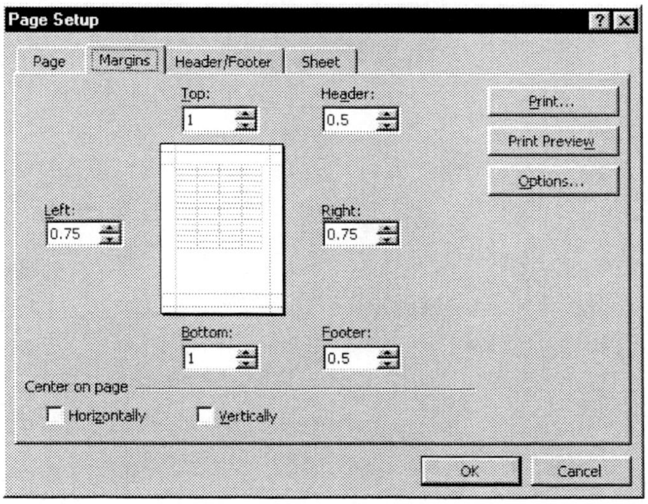

- Click in the appropriate text box, then type a new margin setting.
- Click the OK button.

Changing Paper Type

To change paper type and orientation:

- Display the Page Setup dialog box.
- Click the Page tab to display the following:

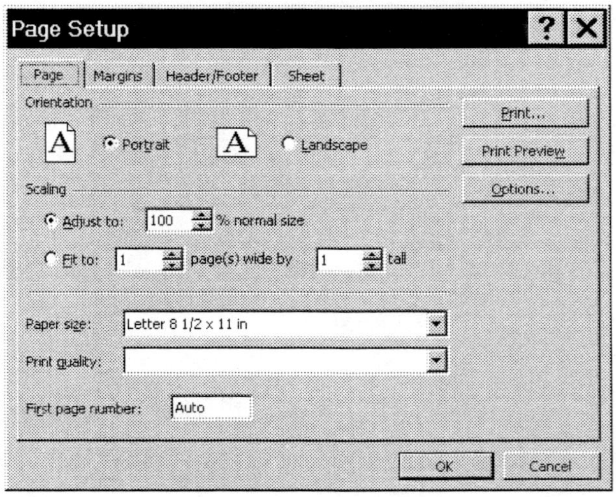

- In the Orientation section, click Portrait to print the worksheet vertically; click Landscape to print the worksheet horizontally.
- Click the OK button.

Inserting and Removing Page Breaks

Excel will automatically insert a hard page break at the bottom of each page, based on the paper type and orientation. You can also add a hard page break by selecting a cell, then clicking Page Break in the Insert menu. Page breaks are inserted directly above the active cell and display as dotted lines. You delete page breaks by positioning the selector in the cell below the page break, and clicking Remove Page Break in the Insert menu.

Saving Worksheet Data to Web Pages

To save worksheet data to a Web page:

- Select the range of cells you want to include on the Web page.

  NOTE: Don't forget to include row and column labels in the range you select.

- Select Save as HTML in the File menu to display the following Internet Assistant's first dialog box:

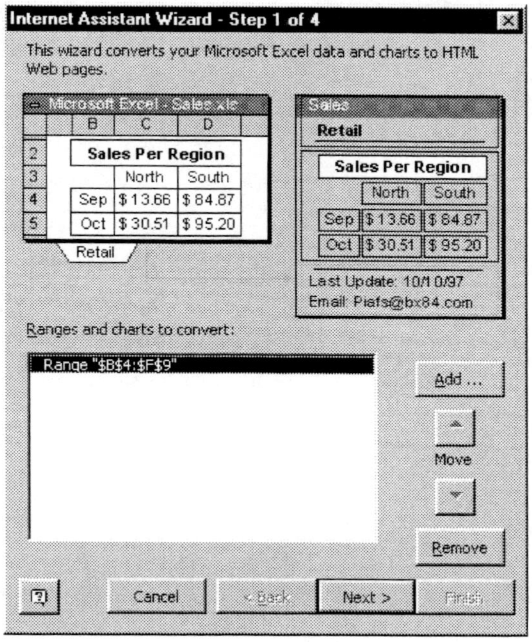

In the Ranges and charts to convert box, Excel displays the parts of the worksheet you selected, as well as anything else it thinks you might want included in your Web document.

- If needed, add or remove ranges and elements from the list of items to include in the Web document. Then click Next to display the second Internet Assistant dialog box.

  This dialog box gives you the choice of saving your data as a separate Web document, or simply saving it as an HTML table which you can then insert into an existing Web document.

- Click Next to display the third Internet Assistant dialog box, which lets you enter a title and description for your Web document.

- Enter a title and description, then click Next to display the final Internet Assistant dialog box, which lets you specify where your Web document should be saved—on your PC's hard disk, in a corporate intranet, or on a Web site.

- Specify where to save the Web document, then click Finish. Excel saves your data as a Web document and returns you to your worksheet.

  NOTE: You can save a chart to a Web page just as easily as a range of cells. Simply select the chart, then select Save as HTML on the File menu. The Internet Assistant will appear and take you through the same steps as before.

Summary of Lesson 5

Shortcut

To select an AutoShape:

- Display the Drawing toolbar.
- Click **AutoShapes**.
- Select a category, then click a shape.
- When the crosshair pointer appears, click and drag to size the shape at the location you want it in your worksheet.

To specify No Fill for an object:

- Click the object until the sizing handles appear.
- Click **Format** on the menu bar.
- Click **AutoShapes** in the Format menu.
- Make sure the Colors and Lines folder tab is selected.
- Click the Fill Color drop-down list box.
- Click the **No Fill** button at the top of the Colors box.
- Click the **OK** button.

To add a shadow:

- Select the object so that the size handles appear.
- Display the Drawing toolbar if necessary, then click the **Shadow** button near the right end of the toolbar.
- Select a shadow.

To rotate the contents of a cell:

- Right-click the cell whose contents you want to indent.
- In the Object menu, select **Format Cells** to display the Format Cells dialog box.
- In the dialog box, click the **Alignment** tab to display the Alignment page of the dialog box.
- In the clock face, click the point for the amount of rotation you want to apply to the cell contents. Drag the clock handle up or down to the desired angle, then click the **OK** button.

To enter a header or a footer:

- Click **File** on the menu bar.
- Click **Page Setup** on the File menu.
- Click the **Header/Footer** tab.

Shortcut

- Expand the Header drop-down list box, then select the desired option, or select the **Custom Header** button and create header entries.
- Expand the Footer drop-down list box, then select the desired option, or select the **Custom Footer** button and create footer entries.
- Click the **OK** button.

To change margin settings from the Page Setup dialog box:

- Click **File** on the menu bar.
- Click **Page Setup** on the File menu.
- Click the **Margins** tab.
- Click in the appropriate text box, then type a new margin setting.
- Click the **OK** button.

Press **[Tab]** to cycle through the text boxes, and to highlight text box contents.

Press **[Enter]**.

To change paper type and orientation:

- Display the Page Setup dialog box.
- Click the **Page** tab.
- In the Orientation section, click **Portrait** to print the worksheet vertically; click **Landscape** to print the worksheet horizontally.
- Click the **OK** button.

To save worksheet data to a Web page:

- Select the range of cells you want to include on the Web page.
- Select **Save as HTML** in the File menu to display the Internet Assistant's first dialog box.
- If needed, add or remove ranges and elements from the list of items to include in the Web document. Then click **Next** to display the second Internet Assistant dialog box.
- Click **Next** to display the third Internet Assistant dialog box, which lets you enter a title and description for your Web document.
- Enter a title and description, then click **Next** to display the final Internet Assistant dialog box, which lets you specify where your Web document should be saved—on your PC's hard disk, in a corporate intranet, or on a Web site.

Practice Exercise A — Lesson 5

1. Open the file named Sales5.

2. Using AutoShapes, use the third shape in the fourth row of the Basic Shapes to create a border around the two title lines.

3. Remove the fill color in the Autoshape.

4. Rotate the text in cell A10 about 30 degrees upward.

5. Add an AutoShape block arrow in cell G10 to point to the final total. Use the second arrow in the top row of block arrows.

6. Resize the arrow so that the width is about half the width of a cell, and its length fits within one cell.

7. Add a 3-D effect to the arrow.

8. Rotate the arrow downward about 10 degrees. Your worksheet should now look similar to the one shown below:

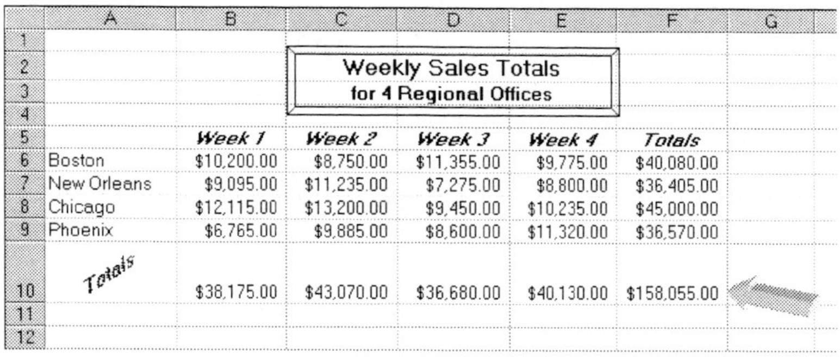

	A	B	C	D	E	F	G
1							
2			Weekly Sales Totals				
3			for 4 Regional Offices				
4							
5		*Week 1*	*Week 2*	*Week 3*	*Week 4*	*Totals*	
6	Boston	$10,200.00	$8,750.00	$11,355.00	$9,775.00	$40,080.00	
7	New Orleans	$9,095.00	$11,235.00	$7,275.00	$8,800.00	$36,405.00	
8	Chicago	$12,115.00	$13,200.00	$9,450.00	$10,235.00	$45,000.00	
9	Phoenix	$6,765.00	$9,885.00	$8,600.00	$11,320.00	$36,570.00	
10	Totals	$38,175.00	$43,070.00	$36,680.00	$40,130.00	$158,055.00	
11							
12							

9. Highlight the range A1:F10 and save it as an HTML file. Remove any other ranges that might appear in the Wizard dialog boxes. (**HINT:** You may need to change the file path in Step 4 of the wizard.)

10. View the HTML file in your Web browser.

11. Close the worksheet without saving changes.

12. Exit Excel.

Practice Exercise B — Lesson 5

1. Open the file named Regional Totals.

2. Add a bevel shape that encompasses cells D16 through F16. Change the fill color to green.

3. Copy the bevel shape so that it encompasses D27 through F27. Drag the shape into the appropriate position if necessary. Your worksheet should look like the one shown below:

	A	B	C	D	E	F	G
8	Accounting	$6,600	$6,600	$6,600	$6,900	$6,900	$6,900
9	Development	$13,700	$13,700	$13,700	$14,000	$14,000	$14,000
10	Marketing	$8,850	$8,850	$8,850	$9,150	$9,150	$9,150
11	Production	$4,500	$4,500	$4,500	$4,800	$4,800	$4,800
12	Sales	$13,200	$13,200	$13,200	$13,500	$13,500	$13,500
13	*Totals*	$46,850	$46,850	$46,850	$48,350	$48,350	$48,350
14							
15	**Chicago**						
16	**Office**						
17							
18	**Department**	***July***	***August***	***September***	***October***	***November***	***December***
19	Accounting	$5,500	$5,500	$5,500	$5,800	$5,800	$5,800
20	Development	$11,600	$11,600	$11,600	$11,900	$11,900	$11,900
21	Marketing	$7,250	$7,250	$7,250	$7,550	$7,550	$7,550
22	Production	$3,400	$3,400	$3,400	$3,700	$3,700	$3,700
23	Sales	$10,600	$10,600	$10,600	$10,900	$10,900	$10,900
24	*Totals*	$38,350	$38,350	$38,350	$39,850	$39,850	$39,850
25							
26	**Los Angeles**						
27	**Office**						
28							
29	**Department**	***July***	***August***	***September***	***October***	***November***	***December***
30	Accounting	$6,000	$6,000	$6,000	$6,300	$6,300	$6,300
31	Development	$13,600	$13,600	$13,600	$13,900	$13,900	$13,900

4. In cell J10, type the words "Highest Total," in boldface.

5. Draw a single-headed arrow from Highest Total so that it points to cell I13. The result should look like the worksheet section shown below:

G	H	I	J	K
$6,900				
$14,000				
$9,150			**Highest Total**	
$4,800				
$13,500				
$48,350		$285,600		
December				
$5,800				
$11,900				
$7,550				
$3,700				
$10,900				
$39,850		$234,600		

6. Create a header that reads Regional Budget in the left section and includes the date in the right section. The center section of the header and all sections of the footer should be empty.

7. Change the page orientation to landscape.

8. Preview the worksheet. Your first page should look like the one shown below:

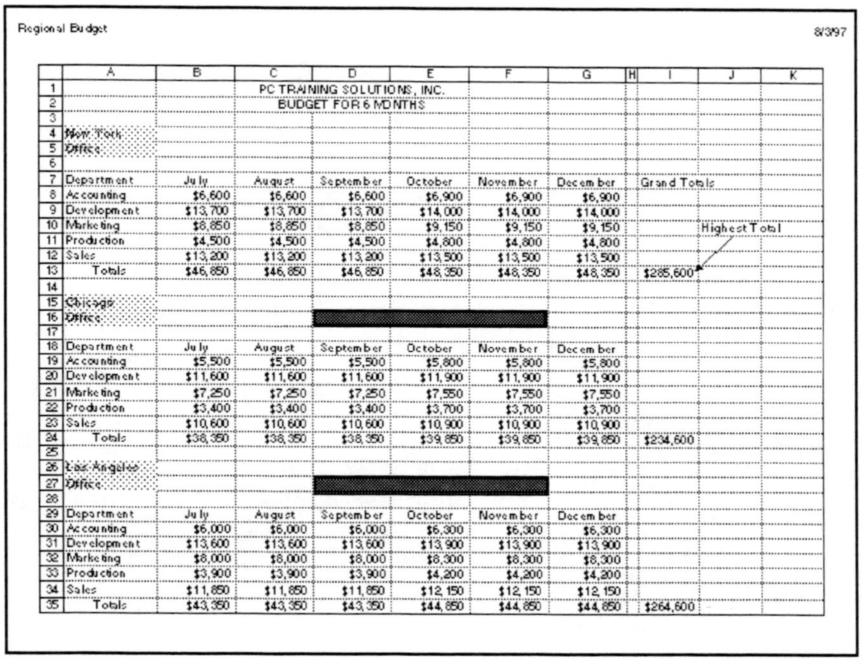

Regional Budget 8/3/97

	A	B	C	D	E	F	G	H	I	J	K
1			PC TRAINING SOLUTIONS, INC.								
2			BUDGET FOR 6 MONTHS								
3											
4	New York										
5	Office										
6											
7	Department	July	August	September	October	November	December		Grand Totals		
8	Accounting	$6,600	$6,600	$6,600	$6,900	$6,900	$6,900				
9	Development	$13,700	$13,700	$13,700	$14,000	$14,000	$14,000				
10	Marketing	$8,850	$8,850	$8,850	$9,150	$9,150	$9,150			Highest Total	
11	Production	$4,500	$4,500	$4,500	$4,800	$4,800	$4,800				
12	Sales	$13,200	$13,200	$13,200	$13,500	$13,500	$13,500				
13	Totals	$46,850	$46,850	$46,850	$48,350	$48,350	$48,350		$285,600		
14											
15	Chicago										
16	Office										
17											
18	Department	July	August	September	October	November	December				
19	Accounting	$5,500	$5,500	$5,500	$5,800	$5,800	$5,800				
20	Development	$11,600	$11,600	$11,600	$11,900	$11,900	$11,900				
21	Marketing	$7,250	$7,250	$7,250	$7,550	$7,550	$7,550				
22	Production	$3,400	$3,400	$3,400	$3,700	$3,700	$3,700				
23	Sales	$10,600	$10,600	$10,600	$10,900	$10,900	$10,900				
24	Totals	$38,350	$38,350	$38,350	$39,850	$39,850	$39,850		$234,600		
25											
26	Los Angeles										
27	Office										
28											
29	Department	July	August	September	October	November	December				
30	Accounting	$6,000	$6,000	$6,000	$6,300	$6,300	$6,300				
31	Development	$13,600	$13,600	$13,600	$13,900	$13,900	$13,900				
32	Marketing	$8,000	$8,000	$8,000	$8,300	$8,300	$8,300				
33	Production	$3,900	$3,900	$3,900	$4,200	$4,200	$4,200				
34	Sales	$11,850	$11,850	$11,850	$12,150	$12,150	$12,150				
35	Totals	$43,350	$43,350	$43,350	$44,850	$44,850	$44,850		$264,600		

9. Save and close the worksheet.

1. Open the file named "Office Totals."

2. Draw a line from the base of cell C1, starting at the middle of the cell, to the left edge of cell B1.

3. Draw a second line from the base of cell E1, starting at the middle of the cell, the right edge of cell F1.

4. Select both lines, then change the line weight to 2 points. Your title should look like the one shown below:

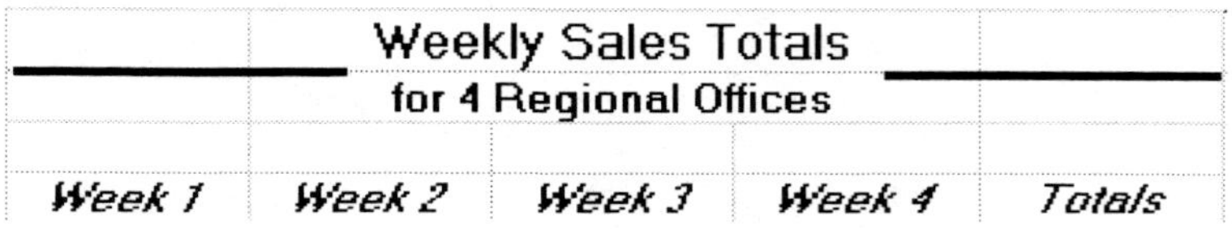

		Weekly Sales Totals		
		for 4 Regional Offices		
Week 1	Week 2	Week 3	Week 4	Totals

5. Add a curved-down ribbon banner so that it fills cells D12 (some overlap is acceptable).

6. Rotate the word Total in cell A9 upward 15 degrees. Your worksheet should look like the one shown below:

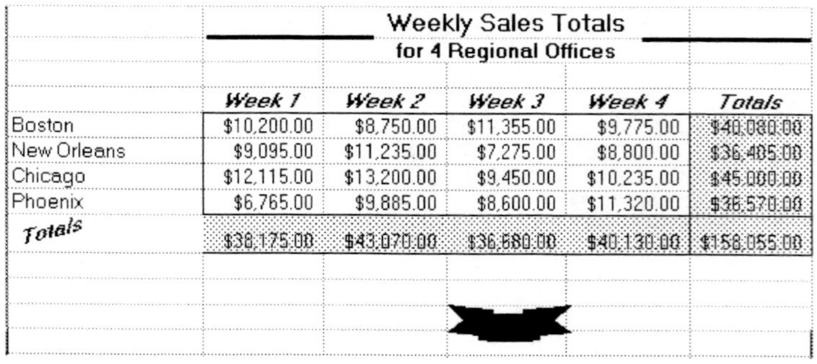

			Weekly Sales Totals		
			for 4 Regional Offices		
	Week 1	Week 2	Week 3	Week 4	Totals
Boston	$10,200.00	$8,750.00	$11,355.00	$9,775.00	$40,080.00
New Orleans	$9,095.00	$11,235.00	$7,275.00	$8,800.00	$36,405.00
Chicago	$12,115.00	$13,200.00	$9,450.00	$10,235.00	$45,000.00
Phoenix	$6,765.00	$9,885.00	$8,600.00	$11,320.00	$36,570.00
Totals	$38,175.00	$43,070.00	$36,680.00	$40,130.00	$158,055.00

7. Create a custom footer that reads "September Totals" in the left section. All other sections in the header and footer should be empty.

8. Preview the worksheet. Its contents should look like the one shown below:

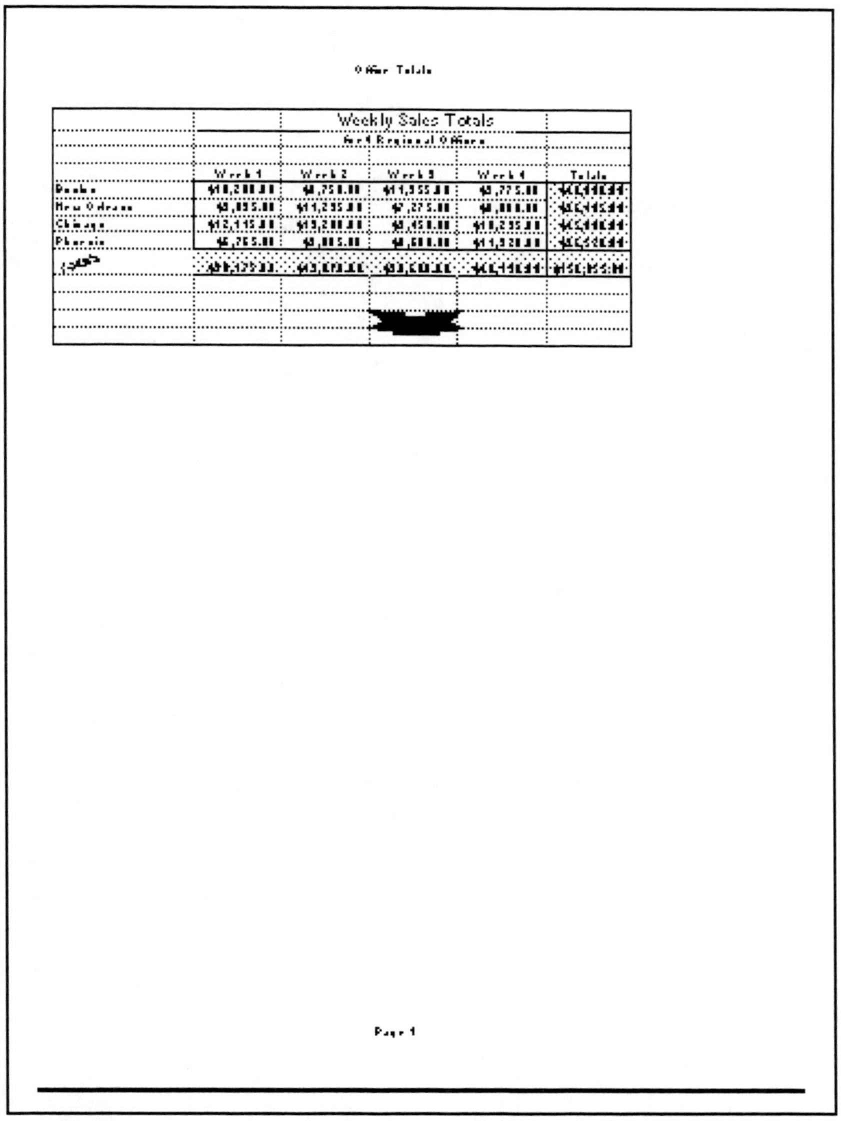

Practice Exercise D — Lesson 5

1. Open the file named "February Commissions."

2. Save the file in HTML format, using the name "Commissions for February."

3. Use your Web browser to view the file, then close the HTML file.

4. Return to the February Commissions worksheet.

5. Use the elbow arrow connector to create a line that begins in cell A19 and points to column H, with the arrow pointing upward in cell H16. (**TIP:** *You will need to drag the yellow diamond portion of the connector to column H.)*

6. Add the ribbon clipart at cell D21. Reduce the size of the ribbon so that it fills only cells D21 through D26. Your worksheet should now look like the one shown below:

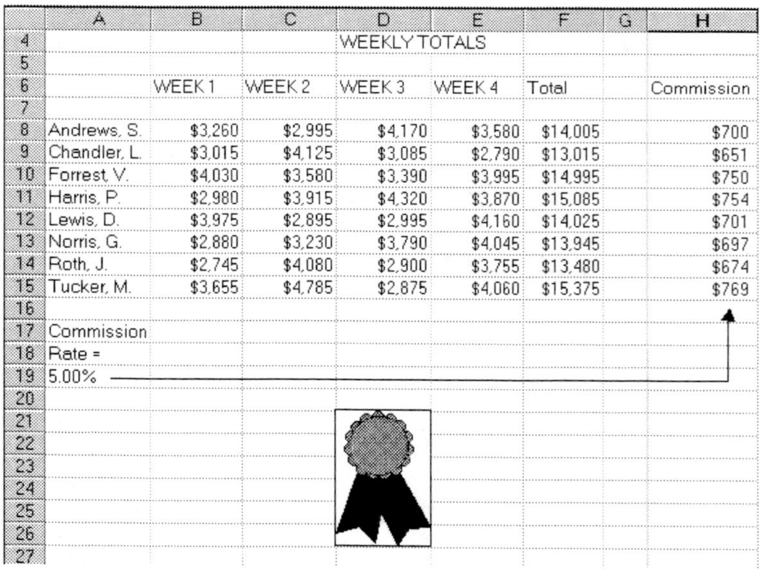

	A	B	C	D	E	F	G	H
4				WEEKLY TOTALS				
5								
6		WEEK 1	WEEK 2	WEEK 3	WEEK 4	Total		Commission
7								
8	Andrews, S.	$3,260	$2,995	$4,170	$3,580	$14,005		$700
9	Chandler, L.	$3,015	$4,125	$3,085	$2,790	$13,015		$651
10	Forrest, V.	$4,030	$3,580	$3,390	$3,995	$14,995		$750
11	Harris, P.	$2,980	$3,915	$4,320	$3,870	$15,085		$754
12	Lewis, D.	$3,975	$2,895	$2,995	$4,160	$14,025		$701
13	Norris, G.	$2,880	$3,230	$3,790	$4,045	$13,945		$697
14	Roth, J.	$2,745	$4,080	$2,900	$3,755	$13,480		$674
15	Tucker, M.	$3,655	$4,785	$2,875	$4,060	$15,375		$769
16								
17	Commission							
18	Rate =							
19	5.00%							
20								
21								
22								
23								
24								
25								
26								
27								

7. Save and close the worksheet.

Naming a Range

Using the Name command on the Insert menu, you can assign a unique name to any range, including a single cell, then use that name to identify it when building a formula or function.

There are certain advantages to naming a range. It is much easier to enter a short, descriptive name when specifying a range than it is to remember the actual cell references for the range. Using a range name in a formula or function can make that formula or function easier to understand. The formula =RATE*HOURS is more meaningful than the formula =D10*B2, even though both may produce the same result. Also, the boundaries of a range automatically expand and contract as you respectively insert and delete entries within the range.

To name a range:

- Select the cell(s) to be named, then click Insert on the menu bar.
- Select Name on the Insert menu.
- Click Define on the Name submenu to display the following dialog box:

  NOTE: If a text entry appears above or to the left of the selected range, that entry will appear as a suggested name.

- Type a name for the range in the Names in Workbook text box.
- Click the OK button.

Range Name Rules

As is true in naming a file, you must follow certain rules when assigning a name to a range.

A name:

- can include up to 255 characters, letters, numbers, the underscore character, and the period.
- must begin with a letter or underscore.
- cannot include spaces.
- can use uppercase or lowercase letters (Excel doesn't distinguish between uppercase and lowercase letters in names).
- cannot be characters that could be interpreted as a cell reference.

Deleting a Range Name

You can delete a range name that is no longer useful without affecting the data in the range itself. Once the name is deleted, any formula or function referencing the range name will reference the range coordinates instead.

To delete a range name:

- Click Insert on the menu bar.
- Select Name on the Insert menu.
- Click Define on the Name submenu.
- Select the name in the Names in Workbook list box.
- Click the Delete button.
- Click the Close button.

Entering a Function

A function consists of two components: the *function name* and, in most cases, an *argument list*. The argument list, which is enclosed in parentheses, contains the data that the function needs in order to produce its output. When a function contains multiple arguments, the arguments must be separated by commas. There should be no spaces between the function name and the argument list.

You enter a function into a worksheet as you would enter a formula. You select the cell in which the result is to appear, type an equal sign, and enter the function. You can manually type the arguments into the function, or use the mouse to paste cell references needed in the function.

If you have created names for various cell references in your worksheet, you can use these names in functions or formulas instead of references to the cells.

Using the Sum Function

One of the most common functions used in worksheets is the Sum function. *Sum* is a math function used to total a list of numeric arguments.

SUM	
Syntax:	**=SUM(numeric values)**
Examples:	**=SUM(A3:A10)**
	=SUM(B5*.25,C5,E5:G5)

Although you can use a regular formula to compute any total, using the Sum function to perform the same operation is usually more efficient. You can also use the AutoSum button on the Standard toolbar as an alternative to manually typing a Sum function.

Understanding Product Function

If you are multiplying a range of values, or a collection of cell values that are scattered throughout the worksheet, you can use the Product function. The *Product* function is similar in syntax to the Sum function, except it applies multiplication to numerical values rather than addition.

PRODUCT	
Syntax:	**=PRODUCT(numeric values)**
Examples:	**=PRODUCT(A3:A10)**
	=PRODUCT(C5,E5:G5)

Using Statistical Functions

The *Average* function is used to determine the mean or average of a list of numeric arguments. The syntax of the function is as follows:

AVERAGE	
Syntax:	**=AVERAGE(numeric values)**
Examples:	**=AVERAGE(A4:A12)**
	=AVERAGE(B6+10,C6:E6,G6)

The *Minimum* function is used to determine the minimum value in a list of numeric arguments. The syntax of the function is as follows:

MIN	
Syntax:	**=MIN(numeric values)**
Examples:	**=MIN(A4:A12)**
	=MIN(B6+10,C6:E6,G6)

The *Maximum* function is used to determine the maximum value in a list of numeric arguments. The syntax of the function is as follows:

MAX	
Syntax:	**=MAX(numeric values)**
Examples:	**=MAX(A4:A12)**
	=MAX(B6+10,C6:E6,G6)

Additional Formula and Function Examples

Use the following examples as a guideline in practicing and developing your skills in creating basic formulas and functions. Each example is expressed first in narrative form, and then is shown as it would appear as a formula and/or function within Excel:

Add cells F3, G3, and I3:

=F3+G3+I3

Add cells A3, B3, C3, and F3:

=A3+B3+C3+F3 *or*

=SUM(A3:C3, F3)

Add cells C3 and D3, then multiply the total by the value in F3:

=(C3+D3)*F3

Add cells C3, D3, and E3, then divide the total by G5:

=(C3+D3+E3)/G5 *or*

=SUM(C3:E3)/G5

Subtract cell F5 from cell G5:

=G5-F5

Divide cell G5 by C5:

=G5/C5

Multiply cells C3 and D3:

=C3*D3

Multiply C3, D3, F3, and G5:

=C3*D3*F3*G5 *or*

=PRODUCT(C3,D3,F3,G5)

Multiply cells C3, C4, C5, E5 then divide the product by B5, then subtract cell G8 from the result:

=((C3*C4*C5*E5)/B5)-G8 or

=(PRODUCT(C3:C5,E5)/B5)-G8

Determine the average of cells C5, D5, E5, F5, and G9:

=AVERAGE(C5:F5,G9)

Determine the minimum value in cells D8, E8, F8, G8, and H10:

=MIN(D8:G8,H10)

Determine the maximum value in cells A3, B3, C3, G8, G9, G10:

=MAX(A3:C3,G8:G10)

Determine the minimum value in columns C and D. (Columns C and D contain values in rows 3 through 6.) Multiply the resulting value by the product of cells E3, E4, E5.

=MIN(C3:D6)*(PRODUCT(D3:D5))

For a complete list of functions and their syntax, click the Paste Function button on the toolbar and select a function category.

Summary of Lesson 6

Shortcut	
	To name a range:
	• Select the cell(s) to be named
[Ctrl] + [F3]	• Click **Insert** on the menu bar. • Select **Name** on the Insert menu. • Click **Define** on the Name submenu. • Type a name for the range in the Names in Workbook text box. • Click the **OK** button.
	A name:
	• can include up to 255 characters, letters, numbers, the underscore character, and the period. • must begin with a letter or underscore. • cannot include spaces. • can use uppercase or lowercase letters. • cannot be characters that could be interpreted as a cell reference.
	To delete a range name:
[Ctrl] + [F3]	• Click **Insert** on the menu bar. • Select **Name** on the Insert menu. • Click **Define** on the Name submenu. • Select the name in the Names in Workbook list box. • Click the **Delete** button. • Click the **Close** button.
	To total a list of numeric arguments:
	• Select the cell in which the function is to occur. • Type **=Sum(numeric values)**. • Press **[Enter]**.
Click the = sign on	**To determine the mean or average of a list of numeric arguments:**
the Formula bar, then click the drop-down list to the right and select **AVERAGE**. Then select the values (cells) to be averaged.	• Select the cell in which the function is to occur. • Type **=Average(numeric values)**. • Press **[Enter]**.

Shortcut

Click the = sign on the Formula bar, then click the drop-down list to the right and select **MINIMUM**. Then select the values (cells) to be averaged.

To determine the minimum value in a list of numeric arguments:

- Select the cell in which the function is to occur.
- Type **=Min(numeric values)**.
- Press **[Enter]**.

Click the = sign on the Formula bar, then click the drop-down list to the right and select **MAXIMUM**. Then select the values (cells) to be averaged.

To determine the maximum value in a list of numeric arguments:

- Select the cell in which the function is to occur.
- Type **=Max(numeric values)**.
- Press **[Enter]**.

Practice Exercise A — Lesson 6

1. Open Work6-1.

2. Use the Sum or AutoSum function to calculate totals in cells F5 and B9, then use the Fill handle to create all remaining totals in column F and row 9.

3. Assign the name Joe to the range B5:E5. Repeat this procedure by assigning the first name as the range name for the other three salespeople, using Weeks 1 through 4 as the range. (For instance, the range name for B6:E6 would be "Sally."

4. Calculate the average and maximum expenses for each salesperson, using a range name in each formula. For example, the formula to average Joe's expenses might be =AVERAGE(Joe). **TIP:** You can use the Fill handle to fill a formula down a row, and then edit each formula to contain the correct range name.

5. Calculate the appropriate totals in cells F9, G9, and H9. The left and right sides of your worksheet should now match the ones shown below:

	A	B	C	D	E
1			Weekly Expense Totals		
2			For Our Top Salespeople		
3					
4		*Week 1*	*Week 2*	*Week 3*	*Week 4*
5	Joe	$480.78	$411.25	$475.22	$551.75
6	Sally	$499.11	$455.77	$310.15	$498.99
7	Fred	$275.42	$565.30	$307.50	$451.80
8	Isabel	$899.00	$209.25	$279.35	$405.20
9	*Week Totals*	$2,154.31	$1,641.57	$1,372.22	$1,907.74

	A	F	G	H
1				
2				
3				
4		*Salesperson Totals*	*Average Expense*	*Maximum Expense*
5	Joe	$1,919.00	$479.75	$551.75
6	Sally	$1,764.02	$441.01	$499.11
7	Fred	$3,683.02	$400.01	$565.30
8	Isabel	$1,792.80	$448.20	$899.00
9	*Week Totals*	$7,075.84	$442.24	$899.00
10				

6. Save and close the worksheet.

Practice Exercise B — Lesson 6

Open the file named Formula Practice. Use this file to create formulas and functions for the following problems. Where appropriate, use AutoSum to assist you in creating the formula.

1. Place the cursor in cell C8. Calculate the sum of column A, then divide the sum by cell C4.

2. Place the cursor in cell D8. Calculate the sum of cells C3, C4, C5, D4, D5, D6).

3. Place the cursor in cell F8. Determine the average value in cells D4, D5, D6, E3, E4, E5. Multiply the result by the product of cells C3, C4, C5.

4. Position the cursor in cell G8. Calculate the sum of cells A4, A5, A6, B3. Divide the total by C6, then subtract E3 from this result.

5. Position the cursor in cell B8. Determine the minimum value in columns A and B. Multiply this value by the product of cells D3, D4, D5. Then, subtract 70,000 from this result.

Answers to these problems are on the following page.

Answers to Practice Exercise B

1. =SUM(A3:A7)/C4

2. =SUM(C3:C5,D4:D6)

TIP: You can use AutoSum to select multiple ranges. Highlight the first range. Then, hold down [Ctrl] and select additional ranges.

3. =AVERAGE(D4:D6,E3:E5)*PRODUCT(C3:C5)

4. =((SUM(A4:A6,B3))/C6)-E3

5. =(MIN(A3:B6)*(PRODUCT(D3:D5)))-70000

Appendix A — Practice Test

The following test simulates the structure and content of an actual MOUS test for the Excel 97 proficient level. Allow yourself 30 minutes—and no longer—to complete the test. If you would like to view the correct, completed test documents, they are available on the Web at **www.ses1.com/testprep/excel.htm**.

Part 1

A. Start Excel, then open the file named Test1.

B. Delete the earnings data for Region 3.

C. Enter the following data into the range just cleared:

B8:	42250
C8:	36500
D8:	37380
E8:	40070
F8:	36100
G8:	39440

D. Increase the width of columns B through G so that all entries are 11 characters in width.

E. Create a centered footer that prints the current date.

F. Change the left and right margins to .25 inches.

G. Preview, then print the worksheet.

H. Save the current worksheet.

Part 2

A. Open the workbook file named Test2.

B. Move the title lines to column D, then center and bold the text.

C. Delete three rows between the title and the body of the worksheet.

D. Sort rows 7 through 11 alphabetically by last name.

E. Calculate the monthly total for sales representative Adams by entering the appropriate formula or function. Then copy the formula or function down the column.

F. Assign the name RATE to the cell containing the commission rate 5%.

G. Use the range name to calculate the commission for Adams. Copy the formula down the appropriate column.

H. Apply the currency, two-decimal format to all the numeric data.

I. Place an outline border around the commission data.

J. Bold and center the main headings in row 5.

K. Insert the trophy clip art picture. Place and reduce it so that the trophy base is at the bottom of cell H, and the trophy is three cells high.

L. Draw an arrow from the left edge of the trophy to the right edge of cell F10.

M. Save the revised version of the workbook file.

N. Save the file in HTML format, then close the file.

Part 3

A. Open the workbook file named Test3.

B. Select the range that includes the names of the sales representatives, the various computer models, and the sales for each model. Copy the range to the clipboard.

C. Create a new sheet and name it Chart_Data.

D. Paste the range into the new sheet, beginning at cell A1.

E. Plot a basic column chart.

F. Italicize the legend text.

G. Add the following chart title:

Computer Sales **Month of January**

H. Place a shadow border around the chart title, then remove the gray shading in the plot area.

I. Resize the chart as necessary.

J. Print the chart, then save and close the workbook file.

Appendix B — MOUS Proficient Skills

Microsoft has established the following skills and tasks as guidelines to help users practice for the MOUS proficient test. The page numbers to the right of each task indicate where you can find a discussion of the task in this book. Page numbers in boldface refer to Practice Exercises that you can work through to reinforce your skills in specific tasks.

Skill Area	Required Tasks	Pages Found
Charts	• Create, format, and modify charts	47–53, **58–60**
	• Preview and print charts	54–55, **58**, **60**
Creating workbooks	• Open electronic workbooks	**29**, 31–32
	• Enter text and numbers	15–16, **28–30**
	• Enter formulas	20–22, **28–30**
	• Save workbooks	19, **29**
	• Close workbooks	25, **28–30**
Using drawing tools	• Create and modify lines and objects	61–65, **75–80**
	• Create and modify 3-D shapes	63, **75**
Formatting sheets	• Modify cell size and alignment	17–18, **28–29**, 37–38, 40, **44–46**
	• Apply number formats	23–24, **28–30**
	• Apply font formats	38, 40, **44–46**
	• Apply outlines	39, **44–45**
Functions	• Use the AVERAGE, MIN, and MAX functions	84–86, **89–91**
	• Use sheet functions	83–86, **89–91**
Internet and Intranet documents	• Save as HTML	71–72, **75**, **80**

Skill Area	Required Tasks	Pages Found
Modifying workbooks	• Delete cell contents	18–19
	• Delete sheets	55, **60**
	• Revise text and numbers	18–19
	• Copy and move data	36–37, **44–46**
	• Insert, modify, and delete rows and columns	17–18, **28–30**, 33, **44–46**
	• Use references (absolute, relative)	36, **44**
	• Sort data	40, **44**
	• Rotate text	65, **75**, **78–79**
Printing workbooks	• Preview and print sheets	25, **28–29**, 55, **58**, **60**, **77**, **79**
	• Print the screen and ranges	25, **29–30**
	• Print headers and footers	55, 66, 68, **78–79**
Ranges	• Create and name ranges	17, **28–30**, 81, **89**
	• Clear and format ranges	17, 24, 82
	• Copy and move ranges	24, **30**

Index

U

V

W

X